The Journal
Essays
The Journey from Essex

JOHN CLARE
Painting by William Hilton
in the National Portrait Gallery

JOHN CLARE

The Journal
Essays
The Journey from Essex

edited and with an Introduction
by ANNE TIBBLE

CARCANET NEW PRESS, MANCHESTER

First published in Great Britain 1980
by Carcanet New Press
330 Corn Exchange Building, Manchester M4 3BG

SBN 85635 3442

© *Copyright 1980 Anne Tibble*
The Publishers acknowledge the financial assistance
of the Arts Council

Printed in Great Britain
by Billings, Guildford and Worcester

Contents

Acknowledgments

My thanks are due to the Northampton Borough Council
and the Northampton Central Library for permission to re-
print *The Journal* and *The Journey from Essex* from the
Library's collection of John Clare MSS. And to Mr Munro,
Mr Nicholls, and the staff of the Northampton Central Library for unfailing help over many years. The *Essays* are
printed for the first time, by permission of the City of Peterborough Museum and Art Gallery; I am grateful for the
kindness and enthusiasm of Mr Tony Cross, Curator of the
Museum, his deputy, and the Museum staff. Finally my
gratitude is due to Michael Schmidt of Carcanet New Press
who suggested this book.

ANNE TIBBLE

Introduction

John Clare was born, he himself tells us, on 'July 13, 1793, at Helpstone,[1] a gloomy village in Northamptonshire, on the brink of the Lincolnshire fens'. His father, Parker Clare, was 'one of fate's chancelings who drop into this world without the honour of matrimony'. His mother, Ann Stimson, was the daughter of the 'town shepherd' of the neighbouring village of Caistor. His paternal grandfather, John Donald Parker, was a 'Scotsman by birth and a schoolmaster by profession'[1] who fled the village on the appearance of his illegitimate son.

At the time of Clare's birth Helpstone was unenclosed. Rural England suffered less than the cities from the rigours of poverty, as poverty was then apprehended. Cut off by bad roads, lack of transport, lack of drainage, areas like the Fens remained self-contained and slow to change. In Clare's childhood folk-song and fairs were a still unbroken tradition. In his *Sketches*, written in 1820 or 1821, Clare says that his father 'could sing or recite over a hundred'[2] ballads. His mother, too, had a stock of traditional songs.

The small, frail child, with startlingly blue eyes and fair hair, was self-contained and inclined to be solitary. When he was five he wandered off alone one morning over the common called Emmonsales Heath:

> I had imagind that the worlds end was at the edge of the orizon & that a days journey was able to find it . . . so I went on . . . expecting when I got to the brink of the world that I coud . . . see into its secrets the same as I coud . . . see heaven by looking into the water So I eagerly wanderd on & rambled along the furze . . . till I got out

of my knowledge when the very wild flowers & birds
seemd to forget me & I imagind they were the inhabitants
of new countrys the very sun seemd to be a new one &
shining in a different quarter of the sky still I felt no fear
my wonder seeking happiness had no room for it . . .
night crept on before I had time to fancy the morning was
bye . . . when I got home I found my parents in great
distress & half the village about hunting me . . .[2]

He went to school for three months of each year until he
was twelve. The few pence needed to pay for schooling he
himself earned by helping his father to thresh corn, with a
light flail his father had made. He went first, for two years,
to a dame school in Helpstone. His next school, to which he
walked two miles along the fen road, was in the vestry beneath the tall spire of the village of Glinton.

The boy had one of those memories of a kind now rare.
It was hearsay in 1932 that he 'could get the whole of the
book of Job by heart'. His schoolmaster encouraged him. At
home he read sixpenny chapbooks, *Cinderella, Jack and the
Beanstalk, Robin Hood's Garland* and *Robinson Crusoe*. And
at Glinton school he found Mary Joyce. Mary 'was beloved
with a romantic or platonic sort of feeling If I coud but gaze
on her face . . . I went away satisfied . . . we played with
each other but named nothing of love . . . I cannot forget
her little playful fairy form & witching smile even now'.[4]

Mary Joyce was the daughter of a well-to-do Glinton
farmer. She herself, and Clare's memory of her, were to exert
a deep influence, both conscious and unconscious, on his
poetry and on his whole life. At the age of thirteen he walked
the five miles to Stamford and, for one shilling which he had
'teazed' out of his indulgent father, he bought Thomson's
Seasons[5]. He then imposed on himself a long apprenticeship
in the writing of verse.

But his father became disabled by rheumatism, the Fen
country scourge, and for the next seven years Clare worked
for various employers as horseboy, ploughboy or gardener.
At nineteen he volunteered for the militia, which was being
recruited to repel Bonaparte's planned invasion, but he made
no better a soldier than Coleridge. The raw recruit of 1812,

[10]

taunted beyond endurance by 'a little louse-looking corporal', seized the scurrilous corporal by the throat and hurled him down. A friendly captain saved Clare more punishment than an additional 'guard'.

On his return home some eighteen months later Clare went lime-burning at Pickworth in Rutland. He met Martha Turner, 'Patty of the Vale', the black-haired daughter of the farmer of Walkherd Lodge. Patty joined the Clare family at Helpstone in 1820, just before the birth of Anna, the first of their eight children.

On 16 January 1820, two months before his marriage to Patty, Clare's first book of poems was published by John Taylor, the London publisher of Keats, Lamb and others, and of the important *London Magazine*. The book brought Clare temporary fame. Soon he could list among his friends Admiral Lord Radstock, Mrs Eliza Louisa Emmerson, Keats, Tom Hood, Allan Cunningham, George Darley, H. F. Cary, Charles Abraham Elton, James Montgomery. Lord Radstock, Taylor, Mrs Emmerson and others, obtained by subscription forty pounds a year for Clare. But isolation closed round him at Helpstone as he continued with his writing. After the brief triumph of his first book, *Poems Descriptive of Rural Life and Scenery*, his second, *The Village Minstrel* (1821) failed to sell. In the spring of 1824 he was suffering from pains in the head. He had a 'dark unsettled conscience', due partly at least to his patrons' admonitions against drink and alcohol. His Muse, 'a fickle hussey . . . sometimes stilts me up to madness & then leaves me as a beggar by the wayside'.[6]

Towards the end of May 1824 Clare made a third visit to London. He was anxious to seek help from Dr Darling, physician to many literary men of the day, who had prescribed for him before. He stayed in London about two months – with John Taylor in Fleet Street, and with his patron-friends, Mrs Eliza Emmerson and her husband, at Stratford Place. He met many contributors to the still-flourishing *London Magazine*. He gained some relief from his anxieties by sightseeing with the self-taught painter, E. V. Rippingille, and with Taylor's porter, as well as from Dr

Darling's ministrations; but Clare returned to Helpstone 'little better', on 8 August 1824.

From his *Letters* we hear again of his troubled mind, his 'miserys'. He was beginning to be humiliated by what he saw as failure. He was deeply anxious for his third book, *The Shepherd's Calendar*, to be published; but John Taylor was clearly not enthusiastic. Taylor gave him a blank book, 'The Student's Journal', of the kind used by Edward Gibbon for *his* Journal. This, with printed and dated spaces, was probably a well-meant suggestion to occupy Clare's restless mind. But, as C. H. Sisson has written recently:

> A man who really wants to write poems will write poems. 'Even if he is no better placed than John Clare', I was about to add, but that would put the matter in a false perspective, for Clare was *well* placed to write the poems he did, and he wrote them.[7]

This is true. It is also, of necessity, intellectually heartless.

The small frail boy was by 1824 the Clare of William Hilton's portrait,[8] the Clare of the high forehead and occasionally authoritative words. There had been a John Clare in the seventeenth century who had been Helpstone's literate parish clerk. But the name Clare/Clayer undoubtedly speaks of a long connection with the land. Why then did Clare, almost all odds against, continue with his ambition to write poems? And poems of his own particular kind?

The years 1824–5, even until 1830, were crucial for him. On 6 September 1824 he began to keep the record of his doings and observations in 'The Student's Journal'. This he continued until 11 September 1825. By then he had begun some Natural History Letters which he was hoping – vainly as it turned out – that his publisher's partner, James August Hessey, would publish. He was contemplating a satire, to be called 'The Parish', a series of character sketches, in rhymed couplets, of the new leaders of the village and of those they led. Another satire, started soon after, was to be 'The Bone and Cleaver Club'. Also in Clare's seething mind, anxious for recognition as a thinking writer as well as a 'country' poet, were plans for Essays, and for his Autobiography, which was to include his impressions of writers and artists he had met during his visits to London in 1820, 1822 and 1824.

During this difficult year (1824) his poetic creed finally emerged. As we know, Samuel Johnson considered 'Lycidas', Milton's pastoral elegy of 1637, a 'vulgar exercise'. Wordsworth found James Thomson's style in *The Seasons* 'vicious' – though he meant 'impaired by inherent defect' rather than what the word infers today. There were minor poets of the eighteenth century who maintained the bucolic and pastoral traditions – James Beattie, Robert Bloomfield and James Hurdis. Clare was against both bucolic and pastoral conventions. He was determined to write only what he called 'natural' poetry.

Characteristically Charles Lamb wrote mildly to Clare that in his poems 'provincial phrases' were 'too profuse'. These were the very 'natural' ways of seeing and thought Clare wished to preserve. But agricultural and industrial revolutions were changing even these. Clare could not follow what he called Wordsworth's 'mysteries', nor did he like his 'affected Godliness'. But with these reservations, 'Wordsworth I love', he had confessed. His remarks on Keats's *Endymion*, written between 1822 and 1824, outline his own viewpoint, as well as illustrate his view of Keat's poetry:

> He keeps up a constant alusion or illusion to the grecian mythology & there I cannot follow – yet when [he] speaks of woods Dryads & Fawns & Satires are sure to follow & the brook looks alone without her naiads to his mind yet the frequency of such classical accompaniment makes it wearisome to the reader where behind every rose bush he looks for a Venus & under every laurel a thrumming appollo – in spite of all this his descriptions of scenery are often very fine but as it is the case with other inhabitants of great cities he often describes nature as she appeared to his fancies & not as he would have described her had he witnessed the things he describes[9]

Byron's popular success had not escaped Clare's notice. Burns's social defiance, as well as his use of old ballads, appeared to have conferred what seemed to Clare both immediate and lasting fame. By 1824 he suspected he might have to barter the first for the second.

After his 1824 visit to London he was teased, though with understanding and even admiration, by the Greek scholar and translator of Hesiod and Propertius, Charles Abraham Elton, in 'The Idler's Epistle to J. Clare':

> What thou hast been the world may see,
> But guess not what thou still may'st be
> . . .
> They praise thy worst; the best of thee
>   Is still unknown.
>
> Some grievously suspect thee, Clare!
> They want to know thy form of prayer;
> Thou dost not cant, and so they stare
>   And smell free-thinking;
> They bid thee of the devil beware,
>   And vote thee sinking . . .[10]

What was the 'best' that Charles Elton saw? Why, in spite of the failure of *The Village Minstrel* in 1821 did Clare set out to finish, not what he knew might please patrons and publisher, but the long poem in 'plain homespun verse' 'The Parish'? In *The Parish Register* (1807), *The Village* (1783) and *The Borough* (1810), George Crabbe wrote, Clare thought, 'like a majistrate distraining for rent'. *The Parish Register* came from a clergyman's armchair, even from his pulpit. The poem Clare finished, also in rhymed couplets, soon after 1824, was 'written under the pressure of heavy distress with embittered feelings' and in 'a state of anxiety and oppression almost amounting to slavery'. Its attitude to human attributes is completely unlike Crabbe's kindly yet strict, assured condescension and moral certitude. As with *The Midsummer Cushion*, Clare tried to have 'The Parish' published locally by a Peterborough printer. The poem related how the 'old vicar'

> His chiefest pleasure charity possest
> In having means to make another blest

> now was gone; as was

The good old fame the farmers earned of yore
That made as equals not as slaves the poor

Justice Terror was new, whose

Gifts at Christmas time are yearly given
No doubt as toll fees on the road to heaven

Also new were farmer Bigg, proud farmer Cheetum, Dandy
Flint, young Bragg, Old Saveall, as well as Constable, Stew-
ards, Overseers, and Ranter priests 'with learning just enough
to sign a name'; and all these new people were after 'money-
catching'. The old herbal village doctress had given way to
'Dr Urine'. There were politicians, with election 'lies' piling
up 'confusion'.

Clare claimed that each picture was 'faithful', 'each censure
just'. His poem may be seen as unrealistic, even mistaken.
Many historians point out that because of enclosure, intensive
farming and the industrial revolution, standards of living for
the English agricultural poor were in general rising. But facts
about injustice in *The Village Labourer 1760–1832*[11] have still
to be proved inaccurate.

Of the Essays which Clare drafted between 1822 and 1830,
all are without fair copies and are often unfinished. They are
on such subjects as 'The Pleasant Art of Money Catching',
'Pretention & Parade', 'Criticism & Fashion', 'Apology for
the Poor'. Only the one on 'Popularity in Authorship' was
printed in his lifetime.[12] Clare may have been aware that the
satire of 'The Parish' was not his genre. He tried his hand at
burlesque in 'The Bone & Cleaver Club' and in five 'Letters
from a Green Grocers wife to her son at School'. These
'Letters' are ludicrously spelt and experimental, like 'The
Bone & Cleaver Club'. The fragments of this consist of
speeches by members of the many working-men's clubs and
mutual benefit societies which were springing up at the time.

The Essays, or parts of Essays, which follow in this book
throw considerable light on what, in this crucial period,
preoccupied Clare when he was not writing poems. Their
subjects are interwoven – 'False appearances', 'Affectation',
'Happiness', 'Industry', 'Pride', 'Honesty', 'Honour' – as
well as those cited above. He was flailing his complex mind

in an attempt almost to dissect traditional human attitudes and attributes and to examine current ones. He was searching his mind in a prolonged effort to quell restlessness under apparent failure, to learn if possible to control a relentless, too unswerving self. In a very different way from either Shelley or Blake, Clare was deeply aware of human complexity. In this he was ahead of what is called romanticism or idealism.

In the Essays, too, he seems to struggle with an almost overwhelming sense of guilt: guilt about not earning enough by his writing to provide effectively for his family. Yet at this very time he was determining to continue: in the essay 'On Industry' he depicts the 'simple old man' still 'expecting money to be found', 'looking for his luck with unremitting assuidity' [sic]. In the old man's son is revealed his own 'anxiety to please', a 'fear to offend' hovering in his mind as weakness or stupidity. 'On Pride' reveals his shame at his family's present poverty.

At haytime and harvest in the 1820s he worked at labouring. But more and more he took long walks in the fields in an effort to reach peace of mind. Before he married did he drink too much and run after girls? Like his friend Charles Lamb, by 1824 he could not 'take' much drink. His well-meaning mentors, the publishers Taylor and Hessey, his rich patron Lord Radstock, even Mrs Emmerson, plied him with the devotional books he mentions in the Journal, and chid him incessantly, often from hearsay, attributing his 'illness' to bad habits and lack of sobriety. The truth about all this, as about his marital fidelity to his wife Patty, is still far from clear.

Undoubtedly there was an intellectual, 'getting-on', ambitious background in the men of Clare's family. He, John, was failing in so many respects. What I want to convey is a sketch of subtleties in Clare's Essays, fragmentary and uncorrected as these are. They await, as does Clare's mind and his whole achievement, a more profound study than the sketch given here.

In Robert Redfield's book *The Primitive World and its Transformations* (1953), the author's thesis is that two differing

types of personality became separated after urban specialis-
ation set in. Redfield calls one a country personality, the
other a city personality. By the word 'personality' I think he
means more what the individual makes of personality – which
is now termed 'character'. The persistent country personality
– character – sets small store on the assumption of power or
wealth; prefers stability to change; refuses to move city-ward
and often stays in one loved place for life. For the countryman in a fluctuating, bigger and more complex world, individual life can have, as Kenneth Richmond writes in *Poetry
and the People* (1947) one magnificent advantage – perma-
nency, constancy. The countryman has little use for war and
war's violence for whatever freedoms. He values 'honesty',
'loyalty', sexual and social faithfulness; he sees pleasure or
happiness as not altogether separable from toil and care and
work; he emphasises, talks openly about, values such as
'freedom', 'liberty' as human aims for which men over the
centuries have striven. Whether or not Redfield's and Professor Richmond's theses have validity, Clare's character-pat-
tern and thought approach those of a 'country personality'.
He had even less capacity than Chatterton or Cowper to
secure payment for his work, whether poetry or prose. Editor after editor of the Christmas books called *Annuals* took
what Clare offered them, recompensing him only with a copy
of the volume. There is a draft letter of 1828 among the
Peterborough MSS begging Tom Hood to ask one publisher
to send whatever he thinks Clare's contribution 'worthy of':
with an income that grew less and less and with four children
already, he could not 'afford to write for nothing'.

Power, influence, greed or money-catching, he didn't, or
wouldn't, understand. What he cared about is stated often,
in Essays, letters and poems: 'Mind alone is the sun of earth';
'truth is the integrity of action' (a quotation from Mon-
taigne?); among the Essays: 'Is it beggarly to be beholden for
a few shillings weekly to the parish . . . & honourable to be
pensioned for thousands on the overburdened parish of the
country?'; to his children: 'look upon your inferiors with
respect'. When, in 1849, he had been eight years in his second
'prison', he wrote to his eldest son Fred, already dead:

[17]

. . . keep the Commandments – not like a Hypocrite but a Man 'Love Truth' – fear God & Honour the king this is from your bible & not my own Words – they are Plagarisms from the Scriptures – Read them – & think Fred – for yourself . . .[13]

Down the vistas of time scanned by his comprehensive, non-political mind, he saw clearly that not all change, especially that made primarily for personal or national profit, is for the advancement of human spiritual progress. Many poems of the 1820s are concerned with the changes for the countryman which enclosure wrought on the countryside and on the class outlook exacerbated by these changes. Between 1820 and 1837 his poems are concerned with ancient folk-council meeting-places, like Langley Bush, about the gathering of wood, herbs, nuts, fruits and berries, rights lost to the village community which was itself changing irrevocably. By 1980 we are more aware of the pitfalls of technical change. In 1824 the ancient pool near Helpstone called Swordy Well was a limpid spring; in 1940 a fetid refuse dump; by 1980 a quarry, barren of vegetation.

Other poems of this period praise the leisured work-play of agricultural life, an identification accepted by Cecil Sharp, Redfield, Professor Kenneth Richmond and others. Romanticised by distance yet not wholly false, it lingers in the term 'Merry England'. Whatever enclosure achieved in wealth and efficiency, for the first forty years of his life Clare watched at close quarters 'Merry England' change for ever.

'The Parish', 'The Bone and Cleaver Club', the unfinished autobiography of 1824 and the earlier 'Sketch of my Life' (1821), even the innocuous 'Journal' – all these stood little chance of publication, or even of favourable scrutiny from Clare's mentors. They thought him mistaken, emotionally errant. Clare was trapping himself more tightly than circumstances had trapped him. He might rid himself of what Kenneth Richmond called his 'anxious lust for private immortality', his hankerings for 'present' fame. By 1825 he had turned, consciously or subconsciously, to a justice he trusted Time alone to confer:

real excellence must be its own creator . . . & must *make*

its admirers willing converts from its own powerful con-
ceptions & not yield to win them by giving way to their
opinions . . .[14]

He wrote little more about personal 'joy' and 'liberty' until
he was in St Andrew's asylum, 'cooped up in this Hell of a
Madhouse', as he wrote to Eliza Phillips in 1841. But with
a tenacity that from the point of view of the 'sane' could be
dangerously rigid, throughout the 1820s he held on to what
from the days of his first protests at Taylor's strictures against
'coarse' dialect words, he insisted on calling 'natural' writing.
Folk poetry, remembered from ballads, he saw as having
been smothered beneath what, since Classical days, had been
acknowledged—by literary judgment only—as poetry. He
was against the 'pomp' of images and the 'falsity' of clever-
ness. His conviction had grown that if popular poetry had
not been debased, if publishers since Caxton had printed
only the 'natural', the 'honest' and the unpretentious, there
need have grown up no cleavage between 'fashionable' and
people's poetry.

If Clare did not belong among the Romantics, that is not
to say he did not share their outlook. Wordsworth's poem
'The Green Linnet' with its romanticised version of that
bird's song, was the kind of poem Clare chose not to write:
its observation was not accurate enough. As David Wright
says in *The Penguin Book of Romantic Verse*, the three poets
most consistently to follow Wordsworth's often suspect advice to poets 'to imitate, and, as far as possible, to adopt the
very language of men', 'were Blake, Burns and Clare, all self-
educated – or nearly so'. Clare, who did not 'follow', was of
that section of the community which, since the days when
John Wycliffe, Wat Tyler, the priest John Ball – four
hundred years before the French Revolution – thought, mistakenly perhaps, that a juster distribution of goods and of
opportunity could result in truer life for all. Of the ideals of
'Liberty, Equality and Fraternity' Clare makes no mention
other than the story, in the Autobiography, of his recruit-
ment. But they were much discussed during his lifetime, as
those who feared his 'free-thinking' knew. The first three
decades of the nineteenth century were a period of the death-

penalty or transportation, for many and often quite minor offences against property.

Clare's library contained many books on resistance to the new doctrines: Thomas Erskine's *Internal Evidence for the Truth of Revealed Religion* (1823), Richard Watson's *An Apology for the Bible* (1796), Sturm's *Morning Communings with God* (1825), Thomas Wilson's *Maxims of Piety and of Christianity* (1822), and so on. With little more than such volumes given by his patrons, Clare's intense mind made what it could of the mystery and 'miracle' of life, whilst agricultural and industrial revolutions rolled on. Other scholars, to whom Clare had no access, would have been Sir Charles Lyell, author of *The Elements of Geology* (1838) and *The Antiquity of Man* (1863). Lyell, Darwin and others were beginning to infer that responsibility for injustice must be man's primary duty. Wordsworth and Coleridge were both over twenty years older than Clare. Coleridge's profoundly subtle mind maintained to the last its passionate childhood allegiance to the Church. Wordsworth, too, defended earnestly the Church establishment. Only intermittently could Clare uphold the Church dogma on which he was reared. By the 1820s Byron, succeeding Scott in fame and popularity, was a rebel in verse, thought and action.

As solitary as De Quincey, what Clare made of his own difficulties of faith in the Christian belief was neither spiritually nor intellectually entire. But essentially he refused to lose hope – in life. In the Essays, reaching toward faith, honesty, and refusal of 'cant' became belief in certain verities. In the harsh midst of his own troubles and of desperate human injustice, there grew a steady belief in Time's 'eternal' goodness. Clare, the countryman who turned ordinary natural details all around him into vividly-lived and living words, also held in his mind two antitheses – independence of mind and a personal vision. There will always be those who admire his writing for quite other reasons. But these two extremes are exceptionally vivid in his prose written between 1820 and 1830, fragmentary as it often is, as well as in poems of *The Midsummer Cushion*, written in that decade but not published until 1979. The earliest of his visionary lyrics, 'Song's eternity' (1820), states a truth not to be denied today, continuing in asylum lyrics of the 1840s such as 'I hid my love'. Half a dozen more continue amid a plethora of jingle as well as lines and stanzas of exquisite description; until in 'I lost the love of heaven above' (1844?) he voices the pentecostal idea of a universal language, poetry's contribution to human understanding.

Clare's fourth book, *The Rural Muse* (1835) – an eighteenth-century title again substituted by his patrons for his own choice 'The Midsummer Cushion', sold scarcely at all. Was Clare reconciled? Not to failure or negation. Yet in the haunting poem 'Decay', in *The Rural Muse*, he sensed a finality, a decay of that 'hope love joy' which he had said in 'The Progress of Ryhme' of about 1824 *were* 'poesy'.

'The Nightingale's Nest', also in *The Rural Muse*, with inwoven rhyme and an accuracy that is itself a lyrical power, cannot be faulted in its observation of bird, habits and nest he records searching for in the Journal. Whether both cock and hen birds sing, as do both robins, is, I believe, a point still unsettled. But oak leaves are always used for the nest and whitethorn or blackthorn thicket the habitat. We recall Coleridge's 'The Nightingale', to which the poet gives a note referring to Milton's 'dramatic propriety' as 'excellence far superior to that of mere description'. But beside Clare's unmistakable 'timid bird', 'clod-brown', 'seld seen', which

> left the hazel bush
> & at a distance hid to sing again
> Lost in a wilderness of listening leaves

Coleridge's nightingale

> perched giddily
> on blossoming twig . . .
> . . . to . . . tune his wanton song

is rather likely to have been a blackcap.[15]

To this large group of distinctive accuracies, Clare went on adding, between 1832 and 1837, more emerald-hard poems[16] – 'Badger', 'Vixen', 'Fox', 'Marten', 'The Outcast', 'Braggart'. Three he called 'The Lout'. There is a half-whimsical identification of himself with the outcast, the lout, and the persecuted, mistakenly accused, badger. All such poems, etched with so much clarity, link Clare with twentieth-century Imagists as much as with his contemporaries. His lifetime's effort to write poems from the unadorned point of view of the perceptive countryman stands alone until the poems of Edward Thomas (1878–1917).

Rejection, in Clare's own day, may have been inevitable as Edward Thomas himself has pointed out. In an urban-directed society few and fewer people were (and perhaps will continue to be) in tune with the kind of poetry he insisted on writing, the only kind Clare *could* write, perhaps. Whether or not what Robert Lowell held is true – that love of nature and gentleness have no future – themes of innocence, constancy, search for honesty, are importances in Clare's poetry. Love of earth without despoiling began in him to increase from 1820. Helpless to alter it, like Blake he watched the process of exploiting the earth for gain begin. But it took until the present century and Edmund Blunden to perceive how in Clare:

> So near . . . are sorrow and joy that they [the later poems] awaken deeper feelings and instincts than almost any other lyrics can – emotions such as he shares with us in his 'Adieu' . . . In this sort of pathos, so indefinable and intimate, William Blake, and only he, can be said to resemble him.[17]

By 1837 the three *idées fixes* most of us have heard about were invading more of Clare's everyday: that his childhood playmate Mary Joyce, the prosperous farmer's daughter who allowed herself to be separated from the labouring seventeen-year-old too shy perhaps to voice his affection, was his first wife. Loyal, practical, unimaginative Martha (Patty) was his second. No wonder his lack of success in what most of us value, perhaps too much, engendered a lack of surety in his very identity, which his strong sense of family intelligence on his father's side aggravated. Occasionally, it was said, he declared himself a bruiser or a boxer – Jack Randall, Tom Spring, Ben Caunt – one of the successful ones of the day whom he had seen on his 1824 London visit. His father is said to have been when young a wrestler as well as a ballad singer at country fair or feast. Strength of mind in an un-wrestler-like physique could make the father's strength of body admired and envied by the son. The third supposed or real delusion was that he 'knew', or *was*, Byron, Gray, Shakespeare. But here we are a little too dependent on the testimony of visitors to his asylums. Tales of a poetic mantle falling on successive shoulders have their metaphorical truth. And reading Clare's 'Don Juan', its very title makes plain that when his mind was clearest he saw through his own problems of identity: 'Lord Byron foh-[18] the man wot writes the werses'. The Essays reinforce his estimate of 'common fame' and of 'honour', as also of 'pretention' and of 'commonsense'. He could not deny the equally common human need to be understood, praised, remembered.

In 1837 Clare became a voluntary patient at Dr Matthew Allen's private mental home at High Beech in Essex. He was paid for by Taylor and the Emmersons. In days of whips for the mentally ill, and straw for bedding, in Britain, he received enlightened treatment with the pioneer Dr Allen. Visiting him, Cyrus Redding reported in his English Journal for 1841 that Clare's mind was not so much 'lost as suspended' through adversity. On poetry, from first to last during his years in two asylums – when he could be persuaded to talk – Clare talked sanely and rationally.

In the spring of 1841 he began two long poems, 'A New Canto of Don Juan' and 'Child Harold'. The coarse honesty of the first comes straight out of Yeats's well-known 'foul rag and bone shop of the heart'. Both poems are sources for the student of insanity – and not only the insanity of poets.

In July 1841 he evaded those 'jailors called keepers', to walk the ninety-odd miles out of Essex to Northborough in Northamptonshire. That grass-nourished journey's relations with those whom he met, pared down to straightforward, common humanness, took him three and a half days. The day after, with a characteristic burst of energy, he wrote, adding a covering note: 'To Mary Clare – Glinton', the prose account of his journey. Mary Joyce, his childhood love had died unmarried three miles from Helpstone whilst Clare was at Dr Allen's.

[23]

During five months at home he continued 'Don Juan' and 'Child Harold', both Byronic chiefly in title. Clare's own shortened fair copy of this second important but very imperfect poem, with stanzas scattered through seven manuscripts, shows a characteristic spring-summer-autumn-winter symbolic form which Geoffrey Grigson first, and rightly, discerned. Since there is not a complete fair copy, the sequence Clare may have intended for many of the stanzas of 'Child Harold' cannot be finally established. But from clear internal evidence as well as external placing, stanzas written in the spring of 1841 *before* the Journey from Essax *must* precede winter stanzas written obviously after his return home.[19] The poem shows Clare's continued struggle to approach a reconcilement beyond the money-grabbing outlined in the Essays and in some poems of the period 1820–32. Such reconcilement no medical science of the day achieved for him or would achieve. He could still write:

. . .
  Smile on ye elements of earth & sky
  Or frown in thunders as ye frown on me
  Bid earth & its delusions pass away
  But leave the mind as its creator free . . .[20]

Since no notebooks went with Clare when in late December 1841 he was hauled from home, resisting strongly this second time, 'Don Juan' and 'Child Harold' must be considered to have ended with his stay at home. At the Northampton Asylum, where he was paid for by Lord Fitzwilliam, he had at first some liberty to walk in the town. His malady passed through brighter and darker phases. Dr Thomas Tennent, Physician Superintendent of St Andrew's in 'Reflections on Genius' in the *Journal of Mental Science*, January 1954, diagnosed Clare's mental state as cyclothymia. In the *Northampton Chronicle and Echo* of 20 May 1964, Dr Russell Brain called Clare's disease cyclophrenia. Whichever it was, it was certainly not schizophrenia.

From the assortment of reading which came his way, Dante, Blake, the Koran, and from the Essays following in this book, fragmentary as most of them are, we learn of his continued preoccupation with concepts of truth, constancy, myth-thought – all now known to be found in what must be called the great religions of the world. He continued to struggle toward this 'natural', mental-emotional harmony that made no compromise on the essentials of human living and therefore no compromise over that important strand in the fabric of human existence – poetry.

W. F. Knight, the St Andrew's steward and copyist of his poems, raised hopes for the publication of a fifth volume. When in 1850 the sympathetic Knight left the hospital, failure and rejection when the plans were not fulfilled must have seemed total. Yet, whatever renunciation Clare was forced into, physical, earthly feeling remained strong. Inner, spiritual-sexual fidelity was part of it. The here and now of visible natural earth were only sometimes 'Heaven' or 'Eden'. Coleridge and Wordsworth in their later, more orthodox years assumed eternity as belonging to a separate after-life. Blake, who, Clare wrote in an isolated prose fragment given in the *Prose* (1951), was 'brave by instinct & honest by choice' found the spiritual world the real. 'Vegetable' existence was unreal. For Clare the earthly 'woods, fields, brooks' remained the real.

He reached, too, a realization that suffering, without earthly hope of release from it, does not, in any possible Plan for Good, make joy impossible. Earthly happiness and sorrow are compounded. In his day and age there was much talk of Eden: eternity in heaven without sorrow – for some. Clare would sometimes call his childhood's happiness 'Eden'. Even when 'mad' his mind could not grasp the strange negation of the doctrine of 'original sin':

> This contradiction puzzles me
>   & it may puzzle all
> Was Adam thus foredoomed to be
>   Our misery by his fall?[21]

After years of imposed guilt about sexual strength of feeling and about 'free thinking', did his final sense of 'innocence' indicate insanity? Certainly the roar and crash of 'heaven's artillery' could, even in manhood, strike nervous fear into him about the terrors of 'Judgement'. From what may seem plenty of evidence Clare's belief in the dogmas of Eden, the

Fall, Original Sin, Judgement Day, might even be thought provable. As much evidence reveals an equally strong, less bleak, intelligent belief, passionately held. From the later 1850s, a letter-draft in his consonant code – where, if anywhere, we may expect to find his deepest conviction – to a real or imaginary Mary Collingwood runs: '. . . Foolish people tell me I have got no home in this world & as I don't believe in the other at any rate I make myself heaven'[22]

He could not, or did not, as Blake, Coleridge, Wordsworth, Shelley could, see the actual in terms of an orthodox spiritual:

> Man earth's poor shadow talks of earth's decay
> But hath it nothing of eternal kin

Another item in his admittedly incomprehensive search was for what Jung in this present century has called the two contradictory halves of love:

> . . . I do not love thee
> So I'll not deceive thee
> I do not love thee
> Yet I'm lothe to leave thee . . .
>
> I cannot hate thee
> Yet my love seems debtor
> To love thee more
> So hating love thee better[23]

The meaning of this poem, as of all Clare's mystical poems, appears simple but is in fact penetratingly deep: the hate in quarrels and the grief and longing in much of love help to make love deeper, 'better'. Clare did not think, as Blake seems to have thought in

> Never pain to tell thy love
> Love that never told can be

that love is incommunicable, though Clare saw to the end reasons for difficulty in expressing love's complexity:

> I hid my love in field and town
> Till e'en the breeze would knock me down
> The Bees seemed singing ballads o'er

The flyes buss turned a Lions roar
And even silence found a tongue
To haunt me all the summer long
The Riddle nature could not prove
Was nothing else but secret love[24]

Clare's ways of knowing love were by its origins:

Love lives with nature not with lust
Go find her in the flowers

You can't be made to feel guilt or shame about flowers or the evening star, though accusations of sentimentality might today be levelled against such an attitude. What Clare seems to have returned to again and again to the end was an obsessive, inconclusive attempt to free human feeling into earthly, rather than heavenly, innocence. And here, content yet uncontent, he had to leave, at the age of seventy-one, the paradoxes of good and evil, innocence and sin, sexual grief and hate, suffering and joy, temporality and eternity.

To the end he wrote in images—noted by Arthur Symons in his *Introduction to Poems by John Clare* (1908) as well as by Edmund Blunden in 1920—which help to show him as the very type of a lyric poet: 'The flaggy lake . . . still as glass', 'ground o' turnips bright green', 'rauk & mist'[25], 'the rawk of the autumn . . . like smoke from a city', 'Flowers . . . brighter than patterns upon shawls'. He continued with innovations in metre such as the unrhymed 'Spring' and 'The Pale Sun',[26] 'Now', 'Hesperus', 'The Dying Child' and 'The Invitation' which was much praised by Lascelles Abercrombie.

Clare was long thought to have no speculative intelligence. His outlook may be called organic – in Sir Herbert Read's sense of that word. Accumulated, materialist learning can fog issues. By refusal of disillusion Clare attempted to outface fear, wrong, misfortune, loss of human hope: 'I fathom my own heart for ways of good'; but how was this Good to deal with predator-cunning, corruption, threat? Yet such yes-saying Clare made the central part of life's and of poetry's continuing natural beauty. Some still see his country poetry as his chief contribution. Others see central, modern importance in his late lyrics; his affirmations link carol, ballad, folk-tradition of poetry with present and future spiritual poetic intelligence.

Perception of Clare's 'organic' feeling-thought has grown very slowly. As Monckton Milnes rescued Keats in 1848, as Sir Geoffrey Keynes did much the same for Blake in the 1950s, so Edmund Blunden rescued Clare in 1920. It is now transparently clear that his simple-seeming fraternity with creature and plant was not any indication of a childish mentality, as John Middleton Murry argued in *John Clare and Other Studies* (1950). The quality of his knowledge and his perception, though the first is not equal in him to the second, makes him much more than the minor poet he has long been considered to be. Slowly his reputation is growing. The Essays, printed for the first time in this book, reinforce untutored yet philosophic ideas that man is more than predator, brilliant calculator, schemer, that human progress may move, not toward perfection, but towards increased wisdom.

ANNE TIBBLE

General note on Clare's texts

Clare's manuscript of *The Journal, The Essays* and *The Journey* from Essex is not a careful fair copy ready for the printer. All three texts in this book are taken from drafts written when Clare was already ill, overworked and frustrated.

In all three I have left his own spelling of words like 'untill', 'ryhme', 'carless', 'recieve', 'majic', 'supprise'. I have also left, and without comment except where ambiguity might creep in, his less usual spelling of words like 'enarmoured', 'origeonality', 'assuidity', 'derisision', 'accidenteoraly'. Where he has obviously missed out a small word such as 'to' or 'a' I have supplied it within square brackets. His tenuous punctuation I have left as exactly as possible; but his often inconsistent single and double quotation marks I have omitted. Occasionally a gap may indicate where one sentence ends and another begins. Difficulty arises, too, over Clare's way of indicating plurals – his final 's' is frequently unclear. His capital and small letters are hard to distinguish, as are 'a' and 'e'. He is not orthodox or consistent about 'were' and 'where', but the sense is usually clear.

AT

Hornet Moth found feeding on the Birdsfoot Trefoil in Royce
wood near Clarks garden – Eyes very black – wings snowy white
– body barred with rings of black & yellow – very vivid but in
flying & coming off with the touch of the finger – not accurately
figured – found in June & this specimen not taken – never seen it
in any collection & named it after my own fancy

The Journal
1824–5

Mon. 6 Sept. 1824   I have determind this day of beginning
a sort of journal to give my opinion of things I may read
or see & set down any thoughts that may arise either in my
reading at home or my musings in the Fields & this day
must fill up a sort of Introduction for I have nothing else
to set down all I have read today is Moores Almanack[1] for
the account of the weather which speaks of rain tho its
very hot & fine
Tues. 7 Sept.   I have read Foxes Book of Martyrs[2] &
finished it today & the sum of my opinion is that Tyranny
& Cruelty appear to be the inseperable companions of
Religious Power & the Aphorism is not far from truth that
says: 'All priests are the same' – the great moral presept of
a meek & unoffending teacher was 'Do as ye would be
done unto' & 'love those that hate you' if religious
opinions had done so her history had been praiseworthy
Wed. 8 Sept.   The rainy morning has kept me at home & I
have amusd myself heartily sitting under Waltons Sycamore
tree hearing him discourse of fishponds and fishing what a
delightful book[3] it is the best English pastoral that can be
written the descriptions are nature unsullied by fashionable
tastes of the time they are simply true & like the Pastoral
Ballads of Bloomfield breath of the common air & the grass
& the sky one might almost hear the water of the river Lea
ripple along & the grass & flags grow & rustle in the pages
that speak of it I have never read a happier Poem in my
time

Thur. 9 Sept.　Took a pleasant walk today in the fields but felt too weak to keep out long tis the first day of shooting with the sportsmen & the poor hares partridges & pheasants were flying in all directions panic struck they put me in mind of the inhabitants of a Village flying before an invading enemy the dogs run with their sleek dappld sides rustling in the crackling stubbs & their noses close to the ground as happy as their masters in the sport tho they only 'mumble the game they dare not bite' as Pope says – I forcd to return home fearing I might be shot under the hedges & wrote 2 letters One to Cunningham[4]

Fri. 10 Sept.　My health woud permit me to do nothing more then take walks in the garden today what a sadly pleasing appearence gardens have at this season the tall gaudy holliock with its mellancholy blooms stands bending to the wind and bidding the summer farwell while the Low Asters in their pied lustre of red white & blue bends beneath in pensive silence as tho they musd over the days gone by & were sorrowful the swallows are flocking together in the sky ready for departing & a crowd has dropt to rest on the wallnut tree were they twitter as if they were telling their young stories of their long journey to cheer & check fears

Sat. 11 Sept.　Written an essay today on 'The sexual system of plants' & began one on 'The Fungus Tribe' & on 'Mildew, Blight Etc' intended for 'A Natural History of Helpstone' in a series of Letters to Hessey[5] who will publish it when finishd I did not think it woud cause me such trouble or I shoud not have began it Recievd a kind letter from C. A. Elton[6] – read the september No of the London Mag: Only 2 good articles in it – 'Blakesmoor in H-shire' by Elia[7] & review of 'Goethe' by De Quincey[8] these are exelent and sufficient to make a bad No interesting

Sun. 12 Sept.　A wet day wrote a letter to Rippingille & to H. F. Carey & finishd another page of my Life which I intend to bring down to the present time as I did not keep a journal earlier I have inserted the names of those from whom I have recievd letters & to whom I have written in cronological order as near as I can reccolect

[32]

I have read the first chapter of Genesis the beginning of which is very fine but the sacred historian took a great deal upon credit for this world when he imagines that God created the sun moon & stars those mysterious hosts of heaven for no other purpose then its use 'the greater light to rule the day & the lesser light to rule the night' the stars also 'to give light upon the earth' – it is a harmless and universal propensity to magnify consequences that appertain to ourselves & woud be a foolish thing to try the test of the scriptures upon these groundless assertions – for it contains the best Poetry & the best morality in the world
Mon. 13 Sept.   Wrote two or three more pages of my Life – read some of the Sonnets of Shakspear which are great favourites of mine & lookd into the Poems of Chatterton[9] to see what he says about flowers & have found that he speaks of the Ladysmock:

> So have I seen the ladysmocks so white
> Bloom in the morning and mowd down at night

as well as my favourite line of

> The kingcups brasted with the morning dew

Tues. 14 Sept.   Continued the reading of Chatterton in search for extracts to insert in my natural history inserted them in the Appendix[10] – I was struck with the many beautifull & remarkable passages which I found in them what a wonderful boy was this unfortunate Chatterton I hate the name of Walpole for his behaviour to this Genius & his sneering & cold-blooded mention of him afterwards when his gossiping fribble had discoverd them to be forgeries why did he not discover the genius of the author- no because they surpassd his Leadenhall forgery of 'Otranto'[11]
Wed. 15 Sept.   Finishd the reading of Chatterton admire his tradegy of Ella & Battle of Hastings noticd a good description of a Thunderstorm in the Ballad of Charity v29 &c &c & a beautiful one of a ladye inserted it in Appendix No 3[12] Chatterton seemd fond of taking his similes from nature his favourite flower seems to be the 'kynge-coppe'

[33]

& his favourite bird the 'pied Chelandrie'[13] the only trees
he speaks of are the oak & elm

Thur. 16 Sept. Had a visit from my friend Henderson[14] of
Milton who brought 'Don Juan'[15] in his Pocket I was very
ill & nursing my head in my hand but he revivd me &
advisd me to read 'Don Juan' we talked about books &
flowers & Butterflyes till noon & then he descanted on
'Don Juan' which he admird very much I think a good deal
of his opinion & shall read it when I am able

Fri. 17 Sept. Began 'Don Juan' 2 verses of the Shipwreck
very fine & the character of Haidee is the best I have yet
met it is very beautiful the Hero seems a fit partner for
Tom & Jerry fond of getting into scrapes & always finding
means to get out agen forever in the company of ladys who
seem to watch at night for easy oppertunitys for everything
but saying their prayers perhaps they are as good as their
neighbours – nay better they do without that fasionable vail
hypocrisy

Sat. 18 Sept. Bought the John Bull Magazine out of
curosity to see if I was among the black sheep it grows in
dullness thats one comfort to those that it nicknames
'Humbugs' I have seen a boy groap in a sink for the hopes
of finding a lost halfpenny but I have been worse employd
then that boy for I have dabbld in filth & found nothing –
abuse without wit is dullness double distilld – the John
Bull News is keen & witty & in consequence entertaining
have writ 5 letters T. Henderson – Rev. Mr. Carey – A
Cunningham – H. S. Van Dyk[16] & Hessey[17]

Sun. 19 Sept. I wish I had kept a journal sooner not of
facts only but opinions of books when one rises fresh from
the reading & thoughts that may rise at the moment for
such a collection woud be an entertaining medley of the
past out of which tho there might be a many weeds one
might cull a few flowers if not candidates for eternity yet
too good to be totally lost in the black unreckonings of
days gone bye Took a walk about the fields a deep mist in
the morning hid everything till noon returnd & read
snatches in several poets & the Song of Solomon[18] thought
the supposd illusions in that lucious poem to our Saviour
very overstrained far-fetchd & conjectural it appears to me

[34]

as eastern love-poems & nothing further but an over-heated
religious fancy is strong enough to fancy anything I fancy
that the Bible is not illustrated by that supposition tho it is
a very beautiful Poem it seems nothing like a prophetic one
as it is represented to be
Mon. 20 Sept.   A very wet day: an occurence has happend
in the village tho not very remarkable yet very singular for
I have not heard of a former one in my day tis a Gipseys
wedding Israel Smith & Lettyce Smith what odd names
these people have they are more frequently from the Bible
then the testament for what reason I know not & more
common from their own fancys then either – the Fiddle
accompanyd them to Church & back the rest part of it was
nothing different to village weddings – Dancing &
Drinking & Wrote a song for them being old friends
Tues. 21 Sept.   The Statute & a very wet day for it the
lasses do not lift up their gowns to show taper ancles &
white stockings but on the contrary drop them to hide
dirty ones wrote a poem on the 'Statute'[19] last year lookd it
over & think it a good one Taylor is of another opinion &
thinks it not but it is true like the 'Lodge house'[20] & others
he dislikes & I shall one day publish them & others he has
in his possession under the title 'A Living Poet's Remains'
Wed. 22 Sept.   Very ill & did nothing but ponder over a
future existance & often brought up the lines to my
memory said to be utterd by an unfortunate nobleman
when on the brink of it ready to take the plunge

> 'In doubt I livd in doubt I dye
> Nor shrink the dark abyss to try
> But undismayd I meet eternity'

The first line is natural enough but the rest is a rash
courage in such a situation
Thur. 23 Sept.   A wet day did nothing but nurse my
illness coud not have walkd out had it been fine very
disturbd in consience about the troubles of being forcd to
endure life & dye by inches & the anguish of leaving my
children & the dark porch of eternity whence none returns
to tell the tale of their reception
Fri. 24 Sept.   Tryd to walk out & coud not have read

[35]

nothing this week my mind almost overweights me with its
upbraidings & miserys my children very ill night &
morning with a fever – makes me disconsolate & yet how
happy must be the death of a child it bears its suffering
with an innosent patience that maketh man ashamd & with
it the future is nothing but returning to sleep with the
thoughts no doubt of waking to be with its playthings
again

Sat. 25 Sept. Read some of the Odes of Collins[21] think
them superior to Grays[22] there is little pomp about them &
much luscious sweetness I cannot describe the pleasure I
feel in reading them neither can I possess discrimination
enough in Criticism to distinguish the different merits of
either both are great favourites of mine yet their perusal
gives me different pleasures I find in the same Vol Odes by
a poet of the name of Ogilvie[23] – 'full of pomp & fury
signifying nothing' they appear to me bold intruders to
claim company with Gray & Collins

Sun. 26 Sept. Took a Walk in the field heard the harvest
Cricket & shrew-mouse uttering their little clickering Songs
among the crackling stubbles the latter makes a little ear-
piercing noise not unlike a feeble imitation of the skylark I
verily believe this is the very noise which is said to be made
by the little swiftfooted bird calld the cricket lark came
home & read a chapter or two in the New Testament I am
convincd of its sacred design & that its writers were inspird
by an almighty power to benefit the world by their
writings that was growing deeper & deeper into unfruitful
ignorance like bogs & mosses in neglected countrys for
want of culture – but I am far from being convincd that the
desird end is or will be attaind at present while cant &
hypocrisy is blasphemously allowd to make a mask of
religion & to pass as current characters I will not say that
this is unversal God forbid –

Mon. 27 Sept. Read in Milton: his account of his
blindness is very pathetic & I am always affected to tears
when I read it the opening & end of 'Paradise Lost' I
consider sublime & just as the beginning & finish of an
Epic poem should be I never coud read 'Paradise regaind'
thro tho I have heard it praisd highly 'Comus' & 'Allegro'

& 'Penseroso' are those which I take up the oftenest what a
beautiful description at the shut of evening is this

> '– what time the labourd ox
> In his loose traces from the furrow came
> And the swinkt hedger at his supper sat'

Tues. 28 Sept.   Wrote another chapter of my Life read a
little in Grays Letters great favourites of mine they are the
best letters I have seen & I consider Burns[24] very inferior to
all the collections I have met with tho they have gained
great praise they appear to me when I read them as the
letters of a man who was looking further then his
corespondents & straining after somthing fine till he forgets
both his boast of independance is so often dwelt upon till it
becomes tiresome & seems more like the despair of a
disapointed man then the content of a happy one
Wed. 29 Sept.   Took a walk in the fields saw an old wood
stile taken away from a favourite spot which it had
occupied all my life the posts were overgrown with Ivy &
it seemed so akin to nature & the spot were it stood as tho
it had taken it on lease for an undisturbd existance it hurt
me to see it was gone for my affections claims a friendship
with such things but nothing is lasting in this world last
year Langley bush was destroyd an old whitethorn that had
stood for more then a century full of fame the Gipseys
Shepherds & Herdmen all had their tales of its history & it
will be long ere its memory is forgotten
Thur. 30 Sept.   Looked over the 'Human Heart'[25] the title
has little connection with the contents—it displays the art
of book making in half filld pages & fine paper—'The
Murderers Deathbed' is very poor the worst thing in the
Newgate Calendar is as interesting – 'Thou shalt not do
Evil &c' is a new version of the old tale of Colonel Kirks
Cruelty better told in history then prose poetry—'Amy
Wilton' is an imitation of the scotch novelists & of course
inferior – 'The Lucrece of France' is good
Fri. 1 Oct. 1824   Had a new will made as the old one was
not right proving nothing that I wishd & everything
contrary—this I dont like I leave C. Mossop[26] E. T. Artis[27]
& J. A. Hessey Executors & all monies arising from book

[37]

profits &c in their trust with that in the funds & whatever
may be put out to Interest the money in the funds to be
drawn out & shared equally among my children when the
youngest is 21 I dont understand the expression in it of my
'Sons & daughters & their respective Representatives' –
shall have it alterd—it was signed by W. Bradford &
Taylor
Sat. 2 Oct. Read the poems of Conder[28] over a second
time like some of them very much there is a many quiet &
unpretending beautys among them the Imitations of the
Psalms are good the Ode to the Nightingale is good but the
expression Sir Nightingale is bad & spoils it – The principal
poem is like many such attempts poor the best poems on
religion are those found in the Scriptures which are
inimitable & therefor all imitations cannot but be inferior –
the first Sonnet on Autumn is a good one & the Song
'Twas not when early flowers was springing' is beautiful I
am much pleasd with many more which I shall read anon
Sun. 3 Oct. Began to read again the Garden of Florence
by Reynolds[29] it is a beautiful simple tale with a few
conseits it begins prettily 'In the fair city of Florence there
did dwell' & ends sweetly

> The lonly nightingale & watching star
> At eve for ever their companions are

there is a many beautys in it
'The Romance of Youth' is too romantic that is the
youth it describes is not a general character – yet there are
several beautys in it of true poesy the redcap is a beautiful
comparison – 'Itself a featherd flower'[30] the comparing the
white stem of the Birch to a serpent is bad taste somthing
like the serpents wreathing round the artificial trees in
Vauxhall gardens – Verse 32 about the kingfisher turns on a
conseit & Verse 66 about the fairys bodice is a worse
conseit still & 'May the rose of months the violet of the
year' is very pretty the volume is full of beautys of the best
sort – the verse about the two children is another addition
to the many from Chantrys monument[31] let C. Mossop
take my new Will home with him for lawyer Taylor to
alter – read in the testament the Epistle of St. John I love

that simple hearted expression of little childern it breaths of brotherly affection & love

Mon. 4 Oct. I have again reflected over my new will & I believe the expression of 'and their respective legal representatives' is wrong so I shall alter it as soon as it is returnd – I had several memorandums which I intended to have inserted in the will but I was told it woud cost too much in proving if it was long so I will insert them in the Appendix No 4³² that my desires may be known & as I anxiously hope attended too tho it often happens otherwise theres little trust in the world to leave faith behind us upon promises

Tues. 5 Oct. One can scarcly trust fame on credit in these days of misrepresentation and deception this morning a Play Bill was thrown into my house with this pompous Blunder on the face of it

THEATRE MARKET DEEPING
On Thursday Evening October 7, 1824 Will be presented
the popular new Comedy (never acted here) calld
'Pride shall have a fall or the Twentieth Huzzar'
written by the Rev. G. Groby and now performing
at the Theatre Royal Covent Garden with
increasd Attraction & Applause – in the Times Telescope

In the Times Telescope they rechristened me Robert Clare there went the left wing of my fame

Wed. 6 Oct. Recieved the London Magazine by my friend Henderson who brought it from town with him a very dull No. the worst of magazines is waste paper repetitions for humbug is the Editor of them all in the June No Dequincey had a paper on 'False distinctions' which contended quite right enough that women had an inferior genius to men in July 'Surrey³³' put up a little clever petition against it which read very well but provd nothing in the lion's head a little unknown stuck a letter to Ed: on the same side in August another popt a plea for female genius between the two opinions of middling stuff in September 'Surrey' popt in another push for his opinion & in October the middling middle one is pushing a go

[39]

between again when will it end – the article on Byron
carries ignorance on the face of it—recievd a letter from
Carey

Thur. 7 Oct.   Got a parcel from London 'Elton's Brothers'
& Allens' Grammer[34] gifts of the Authors & Erskines
Internal Evidences of Religion[35] the Gift of Lord Radstock
one of my best friends a very sensible book this passage
struck me which I first opend To walk without God in the
world is to walk in sin & sin is the way of danger. Men
have been told this by their own consciences & they have
partially & occasionally believd it but still they walked on –
too true – Recievd 3 letters from Vandyk Mrs Emmerson –
& Hessey – Done nothing

Fri. 8 Oct.   Very ill today & very unhappy my three
Childern are all unwell had a dismal dream of being in hell
this is the third time I have had such a dream – as I am
more & more convinced that I cannot recover I will make a
memorandum of my temporary conserns for next to the
Spiritual they ought to come & be attended to for the sake
of those left behind I will insert them in No 5 of the
Appendix[36] – Neglect is the rust of life that eateth it away
& layeth the best of minds fallow & maketh them desert –
Done nothing

Sat. 9 Oct.   Observed today that the Swallows are all gone
when they went I know not saw them at the beginning of
the week a white one was seen this season by Mr Clark in
the fields while out ashooting – Patty has been to Stamford
& brought me a letter from Ned Drury who came from
Lincoln to the Mayors Feast on thursday it revives old
reccolections poor fellow he is an odd one but still my
reccolections are inclind in his favour – what a long way to
come to the Mayors Feast I woud not go one Mile after it
to hear the din of knives & forks & to see a throng of
blank faces about me chattering & stuffing 'that boast no
more expression than a muffin'

Sun. 10 Oct.   A wet day have finished the life of Savage[37]
in Johnsons Lives of the Poets[38] it is a very interesting
piece of biography but the critisisms are dictated by
friendship that too often forgets judgment ought to be one
of the company to leave this & turn to the Life of Gray

[40]

what a contrast it almost makes the mind disbelieve
criticism & to fancy itself led astray by the opinions of
even the wisest of men – I never take up Johnsons lives but
I regret his beginning at the wrong end first & leaving out
those beautiful minstrels of Elizabeth – had he forgot that
there had been such poets as Spenser Drayton Suckling &c
&c but it was the booksellers judgment that employd his
pen & we know by experience that most of their judgments
lie in their pockets – so the Poets of Elizabeth are still left
in cobwebs & mystery Read in the afternoon Erskine's
Evidences of revealed Religion & find in it some of the best
reasoning in favour of its object I have ever read I think a
doubting Christian may be set right at a first perusal & a
reasoning Deist loose Doubts sufficient to be half a
Christian in some of the arguments & a whole one ere he
get to the end

Mon. 11 Oct. I have been dipping into The Miserys of
Human Life[39] here & there the petty troubles are whimsical
enough & the thing is a novel one which is sufficient to
ensure success now & I understand it ran thro a many
editions & that the Authors made £1,500 by it clear profit
– so much for fashion Collins's poems woud not pay for
the printing & the price Milton got for Paradise Lost is
well known so fashion's taste is still the same her outside
only alters – out upon her foolery

Tues. 12 Oct. Began to learn a poor lame boy the
common rules of arithmetic & find him very apt & willing
to learn

Began an Enquirey into the life of Bloomfield[40] with the
intention of writing one & a critisism on his genius &
writings a fellow of the name of Preston[41] pretended to
know a great deal about him but I must enquire into its
authenticity Capel Loft[42] did not improve on the account
given by his brother George by altering it – Editors often
commit this fault

Wed. 13 Oct. Feel rather worse lookd over the Magazine
for amusement for Magazines are the best things in
Literature to pass away a mellancholy hour their variety &
the freshness of their subjects wether good or bad never fail
of amusement to reccomend them Blackwood has had a

[41]

hard hit on Taylor there is no more Editor Scotts at present
to check them

The letter on Macadamizing is good – the Review on
Walladmor[43] is 30 pages long I wish Dequincey had better
subjects for his genius tho there is some parts of the novel
that seems alive with action

Thur. 14 Oct. Wrote a letter to Lord Radstock – Read
some passages in the Poems of Tannahill[44] some of his
Songs are beautiful particularly 'Loudon's bonny woods &
braes' 'We'll meet beside the dusky glen' & 'Jessey' his
poems are poor & appear as if they were written by
another—The Scotch poets excel in song-writing because
they take their images from common life were nature exists
without affectation

Fri. 15 Oct. Read in Eltons Poems some passages in The
brothers are very good & appear to be the utterance of
feeling the small poems are middling 'Rob Roy' & 'A
Father's reverie' are two of the best the epithet 'virgin
voice' is odd & this line sounds namby pambily '&
therefore love I thee' there is a pleasant sound lingers on
the ear whilst reading these lines:

> – the bare trees with crashing boughs aloft
> Rock & re-echo & at whiles are hushd
> I commune with my spirit & am still

Sat. 16 Oct. Wrote 2 more pages of my life find it not so
easy as I at first imagind as I am anxious to give an
undisguisd narrative of facts good & bad in the last sketch
which I wrote for Taylor I had little vanitys about me to
gloss over failing which I shall now take care to lay bare
for readers if they ever are publishd to comment upon as
they please in my last 4 years I shall give my likes &
dislikes of friends & acquaintances as free as I do of myself

Sun. 17 Oct. Receivd a letter from Mrs Gilchrist[45] – read
some passages in my Shakspear took a walk the hedges
look beautiful with their crimson hips bright red awes &
glossy sloes lookd into the poems of Coleridge Lamb &
Loyde[46] Coleridge's monody on Chatterton is beautiful but
his sonnets are not happy ones they seem to be a labour
after exelence which he did not reach some of those by his

[42]

friend Lloyd are exelent & seem to have attaind it without trouble 'Craig Millar Castle & 'To November' are the best with my opinion – Lambs best poetry is in 'Elia' its a sufficient fame in a late harvest – I wish he woud write on
Mon. 18 Oct. Lookd again into 'Don Juan' like it better & feel a wish that the great poet had livd to finish it tho he appears to have lost his intended plan on setting out & to have continued it with any purpose that came uppermost – Don Juans visit to England reads tiresome & one wishes at the end that he had met with another shipwreck on his voyage to have sent him elsewere.
Tues. 19 Oct. Lookd over a New vol of provincial poems by a neighbouring poet Bantum[47] – Excursions of Fancy & poor fancys I find them There is not a new thought in them 4 years ago a poet was not to be heard of within a century of Helpstone & now there is a swarm Roses Early Muse Wilkinsons Percy both of Peterbro Messing's[48] Rural Walks of Exton—Adcock 'Cottage Poems'[49] of Oakam – Bantums Excursions of fancy of Teigh – Strattons Poems— of Abbots Ripton &c &c & all of a kin wanting in natural images &c
Wed. 20 Oct. Workd in the garden at making a shed for my Ariculas – the Michaelmas daisey is in full flower both the lilac blue & the white thick set with its little clustering stars of flowers I love them for their visits in such a mellancholy season as the end of autumn – the Horse chestnutt tree is loosing large hand shapd leaves that litter in yellow heaps round the trunk – the walnutt is compleatly bare & the leaves are tand brown & shriveld up as if scorchd – the elms are as green & fresh as the oaks
Thurs. 21 Oct. Recievd a letter from Hessey – & wrote one – took a walk in the fields – gatherd a bunch of wild flowers that lingerd in shelterd places as loath to dye – the ragwort still shines in its yellow clusters & the little heathbell or harvestbell quakes to the wind under the quick banks & warm furze – clumps of wild Marjoram are yet in flower about the molehilly banks & clumps of meadowsweet linger with a few bunches yet unfaded
Fri. 22 Oct. Read Hazlitts Lectures on the Poets[50] – I admire his mention of the daisy as reminding him of his

[43]

boyish days when he usd to try to jump over his own shadow – he is one of the very best prosewriters of the present day & his works are always entertaining – & may be taken up whenever one chuses or feels the want of amusement – his political writings are heated & empty full of sound & fury – I hate politics & therefore I may be but a poor judge

Sat. 23 Oct. Continued to read Hazlitt – I like his Lectures on the Poets better than those on the comic writers[51] & on Shakspear[52] his 'view of the English stage' is not so good as either they might have remaind in their first places without any loss to the world viz the newspapers for which they was written – his other works I have not seen – Read in Shakspear 'the midsummer nights dream' for the first time – I have still got 3 parts out of 4 of the Plays to read & I hope I shall not leave the world without reading them

Sun. 24 Oct. Recievd a letter from Lord Radstock – finished another chapter of my life read some passages in Blairs Sermons[53] – lookd into 'Maddox[54] on the culture of flowers' & the 'Flora Domestica'[55] which with a few improvements & additions woud be one of the most entertaining books ever written – if I live I will write one on the same plan & call it A Garden of Wild Flowers as it shall contain nothing else with quotations from poets & others an English Botany on this plan woud be very interesting & serve to make Botany popular while the hard nicknaming system of unuterable words now in vogue only overloads it in mystery till it makes darkness visible

Mon. 25 Oct. Old Shepherd Newman dyd this Morning an old tenant of the fields & the last of the old shepherds the fields are now left desolate & his old haunts look like houses disinhabited the fading woods seem mourning in the autumn wind how often hath he seen the blue skye the green fields & woods & the seasons changes & now he sleeps unconsious of all what a desolate mystery doth it leave round the living mind the latter end of Grays Elegy might be well applied to this tenant of the fields 'Oft have we seen him' &c &c

Tues. 26 Oct. Recieved a letter from Allan Cunningham –

[44]

Looked into Pope I know not how it is but I cannot take
him up often or read him long together the uninterrupted
flow of the verses wearys the ear – there are some fine
passages in the Essay on Man – the Pastorals[56] are
nicknamed so for daffodils breathing flutes beachen bowls
silver crooks & purling brooks & such like everlasting
singsong does not make pastorals his prologue to the
Satires is good – but that celebrated Epitaph on Gay ends
burlesquely 'Striking their pensive bosoms &c'
Wed. 27 Oct.   I have been very much stuck with some
passages in the Poems of Aaron Hill[57] with many happy
expressions & original images I have inserted a few of them
in the Appendix No 8[58] he seems to struggle to free his
ideas from the turnpike hackneyhisms of sounding rhymes
& tinkling periods then in fashion for most of the ryhmers
of that day seem to catch their little inspirations from Pope
Thur. 28 Oct.   Wrote a letter to Mrs Gilchrist – read some
pages in Shakspear – turnd over a few leaves of Knoxes
Essay[59] – read Bacons essay on the idea of a compleat
garden[60] divided into every month of the year in which the
flowers bloom – what beautiful Essays these are I take
them up like Shakspear & read them over & still find
plenty to entertain me & new thoughts that strike me as if
for the first time
Fri. 29 Oct.   Read some poems of Wordsworth his 'Susan
[Lucy] Gray' or 'Solitude' 'The pet lamb' 'We are Seven'
'The Oak & broom' 'The Eglantine & the fountain'[61] 'Two
April Mornings' 'Lucy' are some of my greatest favourites
– When I first began to read poetry I dislikd Wordsworth
because I heard he was dislikd & I was astonishd when I
lookd into him to find my mistaken pleasure in being
delighted & finding him so natural & beautiful in his
'White doe of Rylston' there is some of the sweetest poetry
I ever met with tho full of his mysterys
Sat. 30 Oct.   Recievd a present of two Volumes of
Sermons 'On the Doctrines & Practice of Christianity'
from Lord Radstock[62] – he is one of my best friends & not
of much kin with the world – the chrisanthymums are just
opening their beautiful double flowers I have six sorts this
year the claret colord the buff the bright yellow the paper

white the purple & the rose colord—lost one – the jocolat
or coffe color – promisd more from Milton
Sun. 31 Oct.   Took a walk got some branches of the
spindle tree with its pink colord berrys that shine
beautifully in the pale sun – found for the first time 'the
herb true love' or 'one berry' in Oxey Wood[63] brought a
root home to set in my garden – Lookd into the two Vols
of Sermons from Lord R the texts are well selected & the
sermons are plainly & sensibly written they are in my mind
much superior to Blairs[64] popular Sermons & that is not
going great lengths in their praise for Blairs are quiet &
cold & his study seems more in the eloquence & flow of
Style then in the doctrine of religion for the language is
beautiful but it is studied like Dr Johnsons musical periods
Mon. 1 Nov. 1824   Took a walk to Lolam brigs to hunt
for a species of fern that used to grow on some willow tree
heads in Lolham lane when I was a boy but coud find none
– got some of the yellow water-lily from the pits which the
floods had washed up to set in an old water tub in the
garden & to try some on land in a swaily[65] corner as the
horse blob thrives well which is a water flower – Listend in
the evening to Glinton bells at the top of the garden I
always feel mellancholy at this season to hear them & yet it
is a pleasure

> 'I'm pleased & yet I'm sad'

Tues. 2 Nov.   Set some box edging round a border which I
have made for my collection of ferns—read some passages
in Blairs Grave a beautiful poem & one of the best things
after the manner of Shakspear its beginning is very
characteristic of the subject – there are crowds of beautiful
passages about it—who has not markd the following aged
companions to many such spots of general decay

> . . . 'a row of reverend elms
> Long lashd by the rude winds. Some reft half down
> . . . others so thin atop,
> That scarce two crows can lodge in the same tree.'

Wed. 3 Nov.   Took a walk with John Billings to Swordy
well to gather some 'old man's beard'[66] which hangs about

[46]

the hedges in full bloom – its downy clusters of artificial like flowers appear at first sight as if the hedge was litterd with bunches of white cotton – went into hilly wood & found a beautiful species of fern on a sallow stoven in a pit which I have not seen before – there are five sorts growing about the woods here the common brake the fox fern the hart's tongue & the polopody two sorts the tall & the dwarf

Thur. 4 Nov.   Recievd a letter & prospectus from a Schoolmaster of Surfleet wishing me to become a correspondent to a periodical publication calld 'the Scientific Receptacle' what a crabbed name for poesy to enlist with – it professes to be a kinsman to The Leeds Correspondant & the Boston Enquirer the latter of which I remember to have been much pleasd with – in which was a pretty song by poor Scott[67]

Fri. 5 Nov.   Read in Bishop Percys[68] poems the Relics of ancient poetry take them up as often as I may I am always delighted there is so much of the essence & simplicity of true poetry that makes me regret I did not see them sooner as they woud have formd my taste & laid the foundation of my judgment in writing & thinking poetically as it is I feel indebted to them for many feelings

Sat. 6 Nov.   Took a walk in the fields the oaks are beginning to turn reddish brown & the winds have stript some nearly bare the underwoods[69] last leaves are in their gayest yellows thus autumn seems to put on bridal colours for a shroud – the little harvest bell is still in bloom trembling to the cold wind almost the only flower living save the old man's beard or travellers joy on the hedges

Sun. 7 Nov.   Recieved a packet from London with the Mag & some copys of M.S.S. that come very slowly & a letter very friendly worded but I have found that saying & doing is a wide difference too far very often to be neighbours much less friends – Recievd a letter too from Vandyke – Lookd into Wordsworth Poems & read Solomons Song & beautiful as some of the images of that poem are some of them are not reconsilable in my judgment above the ridicilous I have inserted them in a blank verse fashion in the Appendix No 7 yet the more I

read the Scriptures the more I feel astonishment at the
sublime images I continually meet with in its Poetical &
prophetic books nay everywere about it all other authors
diminishes to dwarfs by their side
Mon. 8 Nov. Read over the Magazine the Review of Lord
Byrons Conversations is rather entertaining the pretending
letter of James Thompson is a bold lye I dislike those lapt
up counterfeits mantld in truth like a brassy shilling in its
silver washings those birmingham halfpence passed off as
matter of fact moneys Elia can do better—the rest of the
articles are motly matters some poor & some middling
Magazines are always of such wear
Tues. 9 Nov. Read Shakespears Henry the Fifth of which
I have always been very fond from almost a boy I first met
with it in an odd Vol which I got for 6d yet I thought then
that the welch officer with two other of his companions
were tedious talkers & I feel that I think so still yet I feel
such an interest about the play that I can never lay it down
till I see the end of it
Wed. 10 Nov. Read Macbeth what a soul thrilling power
hovers about this tradegy I have read it over about twenty
times & it chains my feelings still to its perusal like a new
thing it is Shakspears masterpiece – the thrilling feelings
created by the description of Lady Macbeths terror haunted
walkings in her sleep sinks deeper than a thousand ghosts
at least in my vision of the terrible she is a ghost herself &
feels with spirit & body a double terror
Thur. 11 Nov. Recievd a letter from Inskip[70] the friend of
Bloomfield full of complaints at my neglect of writing what
use is writing when the amount on both sides amounts to
nothing more then waste paper I have desires to know
something of Bloomfields latter days but I can hear of
nothing further than his dying neglected so its of no use
enquiring further – for we know that to be the common lot
of genius
Fri. 12 Nov. Burnt a will which Taylor of Deeping made
for me by Mossops Orders as it was a jumble of
contradictions to my wishes – wrote the outline for another
In which I mean to leave everything both in the copyright
& fund money &c &c of all my Books M.S.S. & property

in the power of my family at least in the trust of those I shall nominate trustees & Lord Radstock is one that I shoud like to trouble for the purpose

Sat. 13 Nov.   Lookd into Thompsons[71] Winter there is a freshness about it I think superior to the others tho rather of a pompous cast how natural all his descriptions are nature was consulted in all of them the more I read them the more truth I discover the following minute descriptions are great favourites of mine & prove what I mean describing a hasty flood forcing through a narrow passage he says

>   – rapid & deep
> It boils & wheels & foams & thunders through
> Snatchd in short eddies plays the witherd leaf
> & on the flood the dancing feather floats

Sun. 14 Nov.   Read in old Tusser[72] with whose quaint ryhmes I have often been entertaind he seems to have been acquainted with most of the odd measures now in fashion he seems to have felt a taste for enclosures & Mavor[73] that busy notemaker & book compiler of schoolboy memory has added an impertinent note to tussers opinion as an echo of faint praise so much for a parsons opinion in such matters—I am an advocate for open fields & I think that others experience confirms my opinion every day – there is two pretty sonnets in Tusser & some natural images scatterd about the book the four following lines are pretty

> The year I compare as I find for a truth
> The Spring unto childhood the summer to youth
> The harvest to manhood the winter to age
> All quickly forgot as a play on a stage

Some of the words in the glossary have different meanings with us – to addle means to earn wages – eddish with us is the grass that grows again af[ter] it is mown – staddle[74] bottom of a stack &c &c

Mon. 15 Nov.   Went to gather pootys[75] on the roman bank for a collection found a scarce sort of which I only saw two in my life one picked up under a hedge at peakirk town end & another in bainton meadow its color is a fine

sunny yellow larger then the common sort & round the
rim of the base is a black edging which extends no further
then the rim it is not in the collection at the British
Museum

Tues. 16 Nov.   My friend Billings told me he saw four
swallows about the second of this month flying over his
house he has not seen them since & he forgot to tell me at
the time – now what becomes of these swallows for the
winter that they cannot go into another country now is
certain & that they must abide or perish here is certain but
how or were is a mystery that has made more opinions
then proofs & remains a mystery[76]

Wed. 17 Nov.   The Chrisanthemums are in full flower
what a beautiful heart cheering to the different seasons
nature has provided in her continual successions of the
bloom of flowers – ere winters bye the little acconite peeps
its yellow flowers then the snowdrop is further on the
crocus dropping in before the summer multitude & after
their departure the tall hollioak & little aster blooms in
their showy colors then comes the michaelmas daisy &
lastly the Chrisanthemum while the China roses

all the year
Or in the bud or in the bloom appear

Thur. 18 Nov.   Read in Southeys Wesley[77] he has made a
very entertaining book of it but considering the subject I
think he might have made more of it the character of
Wesley is one of the finest I have read of they may speak
of him as they please but they cannot diminish his
simplicity of genius as an author & his piety as a christian I
sincerely wish that the present day coud find such a man

Fri. 19 Nov.   Had a visit from my friend Henderson & I
felt revivd as I was very dull before: he had pleasing News
to deliver me having discoverd a new species of Fern a few
days back growing among the bogs on Whittlesea Mere &
our talk was of Ferns for the day He tells me there is 24
different species or more natives of England & Scotland
one of the finest of the latter is calld the Maidenhair fern
growing in rock clefts

Sat. 20 Nov.   Went out to hunt the harts tongue species of

[50]

fern & fell in with the ruins of the old castle in Ashton lawn but found none its commonest place is in Wells in the crevices of the walls but I have found it growing about the badger holes in Open Copy wood got very wet & returnd home – finishd the 8th Chapter of my life

Sun. 21 Nov.   Paid a second visit to the old castle in Ashton lawn with my companion J Billings to examine it – we strum[78] it & found it 20 yards long fronting the south & 18 fronting eastward we imagind about 12 foot of the walls still standing tho the rubbish has entirely coverd them except in some places were about a foot of the wall may be seen it is coverd within & without with blackthorn & privet & surge [spurge?] laurel so that it is difficult to get about to view it I broke some of the cement off that holds the stones together & it appears harder then the stones itself brought some home in my pocket for my friend Artis there is some rabbit haunts it & the earth the [y] root out of their burrows is full of this cement & perishd stone – part of the moat is still open

Mon. 22 Nov.   Lookd into Miltons Paradise lost I once read it thro when I was a boy at that time I liked the Death of Abel[79] better what odd judgments those of boys are how they change as they ripen when I think of the slender merits of the Death of Abel against such a giant as Milton I cannot help smiling at my young fancys in those days of happy ignorance

Tues. 23 Nov.   Some months back I began a system of profiting by my reading at least to make a show of it by noting down beautiful odd or remarkable passages immitations in the poets & prosewriters which I read & have inserted some likenesses [?] of Lord Byrons in the Appendix No 8[80] about which there has been much batteling & ink shed I never saw some of them noticed before

Wed. 24 Nov.   I have often been struck with astonishment at the tales old men & women relate on their remembrances of the growth of tree[s] the elm groves in the Staves acre Close at the town end were the rooks build & that are of jiant height my old friend Billings says he remembers them no thicker then his stick & saw my fathers uncle set them

[52]

carr[y]ing a score on his back at once I can scarcly believe
it
Thur. 25 Nov. Recievd a letter from Hessey I have not
answerd his last & know not when I shall The worlds
friendships are counterfits & forgerys on that principle I
have provd it & my affections are sickend unto death & my
memorys are broken while my confidence is grown to a
shadow – in the bringing out of the second edition of the
Minstrel they were a twelve-month in printing a title-page
Fri. 26 Nov. Went to see if the old hazel nut tree in Lea
close was cut down & found it still standing it is the largest
hazel tree I ever saw being thicker then ones thigh in the
trunk & the height of a moderate Ash – I once got a half
peck of nutts when in the heams [halms] off its branches
when a boy – the Inclosure has left it desolate its
companion of oak & ash being gone
Sat. 27 Nov. Recievd a parcel of Ferns & flowers from
Henderson the common Polipody growing about the
Thorp park wall the harts tongue growing in a well at
Caister the Lady fern growing at Whittlesea Meer & tall
White Lychnis with seven new sorts of Chrysanthemums –
the Paper White the bright lemon 3 sorts of lilac & 2 others
– I love these flowers as they come in the melancholy of
autumn
Sun. 28 Nov. A gentleman came to see me today whose
whole talk was of Bloomfield & Booksellers he told me to
put no faith in them & when I told him that all my faith &
M.S.S. likewise was in their hands already he shook his
head & declared with a solemn bend of his body 'Then you
are done by G-d – they will never print them but dally you
on with well managed excuses to the grave & then boast
that they were your friends when you are not able to
contradict it as they have done to Bloomfield' he then
desired me to get my M.S.S. back by all means & sell them
at a markets price at what they woud fetch he said that
Bloomfield had not a £100 a year to maintain 5 or 6 in the
family why I have not £50 to maintain 8 with this is a
hungry difference
Mon. 29 Nov. Lent Henderson 5 Nos. of 'London Mag:'
from July to November & 'The Human Heart'[81]

Tues. 30 Nov. An excessive wet day – Read the Literary
Souvenir[82] for 1825 in all its gilt & finery what a number of
candidates for fame are smiling on its pages – what a pity it
is that time shoud be such a destroyer of our hopes &
anxietys for the best of us are but doubts on fame's
promises & a century will thin the myriad worse than a
plague
Thur. 2 Dec. 1824 One of the largest floods ever known
is out now an old neighbour Sam Sharp out last night at
Deeping Gate on attempting to get home was drownd
Fri. 3 Dec. Found a very beautiful fern in Oxey Wood
suppose it the White Maiden Hair of Hill it is very scarce
here
Sun. 5 Dec. I have been thinking today of all the large
trees about our neighbourhood & those that have curious
historys about them – there was a Walnutt tree (now cut
down) stood in Lowes yard [of] Glinton of which this is
the history – old Will Tyers now living says while going to
Peakirk one day when a boy he pickd up a walnutt & took
it home to set in his garden were it throve well & bore
nutts before he left the house it[s] present occupier got
great quantitys of nutts most seasons & a few years back it
was cut down & the timber sold for £50
Tues. 7 Dec. Another Gipsey wedding of the Smiths
family fiddling & drinking as usual
Wed. 8 Dec. Found the very common Pollopody on an
old Willow tree in Lolham Lane & a small fern in hilly
wood scarcly larger than some species of moss & a little
resembling curld parsley I have named it the Dwarf
Maidenhair I believe it is very scarce here
Fri. 10 Dec. Began to take the Stamford Mercury
Newspaper with Bradford & Stephenson
Mon. 13 Dec. Bought a Moors Almanack[83] with its fresh
budget of wonderful predictions on the weather & the
times utterd with such earnest ambition of pretending truth
that one shoud think the motto 'the voice of the heavens'
&c means nothing more or less then the voice of Moors
Almanack &c – saw two 'Will o' Whisps' last night See
Appendix No 9[84]
Tues. 14 Dec. A coppled crownd Crane shot at Billings

[54]

pond on the Green – twas 4 foot high from the toes to the
bill on the breast & rump was a thick shaggy down full of
powder which seems to be a sort of pounce-box to the bird
to dress its feathers with to keep out the wet – its neck &
breast were beautifully staind with streaks of watery brown
its wings & back was slate grey the down on its head was
of the same color

Wed. 15 Dec.   Went to Milton saw a fine Edition of
Lenniuses [Linnaeus] Botany with beautiful plates & find
that my fern which I found in Harrisons close dyke by the
wood lane is the 'thorn-pointed fern' saw also a beautiful
book on insects with the plants they feed on by Curtis-
found Artis busy over his 'fossil plants' & Roman
Antiquitys but his complaints of the deceptions of
publishers are akin with mine

Thur. 16 Dec.   Saw Hendersons collection of Ferns which
is far from compleat tho some of them are beautiful –
learnd from him of a singular instinct in plants of the
creeping or climbing kind some having a propensity to
twine to the left in their climbing & others to the right –
the woodbine seems to twine to the left & the travellers joy
to the right but this is not an invariable fact

Fri. 17 Dec.   Recievd a letter from Lord Radstock

Sun. 19 Dec.   Returned from Milton

Wed. 22 Dec.   A coppled crownd hen pheasant shot very
large & colord about the breast & back like the cock but
the head was plain

Thur. 23 Dec.   Recievd a letter from Mrs Emmerson & the
'Observer' after a long absence in France – Wrote a letter
to Mrs E & to Francis Freeling Esq –

Sat. Christmas Day   gatherd a handful of daiseys in full
bloom – saw a woodbine & dogrose in the woods putting
out in full leaf & a primrose root full of ripe flowers –
what a day this usd to be when a boy how eager I usd to
attend the church to see it stuck with evergreens (emblems
of Eternity) & the cottage windows & the picture ballads
on the wall all stuck with Ivy holly Box & yew – such
feelings are past – & 'all this world is proud of'

Sun. 26 Dec.   Found at the bottom of a dyke made in the
roman bank some pootys of varied colors & the large

garden ones of a russet color with a great many others of
the meadow sort which we called 'badgers' when I was a
schoolboy found nowere now but in wet places – there is a
great many too of a water species now extinct – the Dyke
is 4 foot deep & the soil is full of these shells – have they
not lay [lain] here ever since the romans made the bank &
does the water sorts not imply that the fields were all fen &
under water or wet & uncultivated at that time I think it
does – I never walk on this bank but the legions of the
roman army pass bye my fancys with their mysterys of
nearly 2000 years hanging like a mist around them what
changes hath past since then – were I found these shells it
was heath land above 'swordy well'
Wed. 29 Dec.   Went with neighbour Billings to Southey
Wood & Gees Holt to hunt ferns – found none – met with
a new species of moss fern stripd growing on a common
species like the mistletoe on the thorn it is a sort of moss
mistletoe – preservd a specimen – saw a branch of
blackthorn dog-rose & eldern in full leaf all in one
hedgerow – saw a bumbarrel[85] with moss as if building a
nest
Thur. 30 Dec.   Recievd an answer from F. Freeling to my
enquirey wether the charge of a penny is legal at Deeping
office for post paid & frankd letters & Newspapers & I
find that it is for letters but no mention is made about
Newspapers so I am as ignorant as ever on that head but I
will enquire further
Fri. 31 Dec.   Recievd a letter from Hessey containing a
Draft for £20 being the fund money & Earl Spencers half
yearly salary – nothing further about my new poems is
mentioned – wrote to Rev. H. F. Carey – Gatherd a
crowflower in full bloom
Sat. 1 Jan. 1825   Saw a Reciept to mend broken China in
the Stamford Mercury – 'Gloucester cheese softend by
warm water & mixd with quick lime is a good cement for
China-ware &c &c – Newspapers have been famous for
Hyperbole & the Stamford Mercury has long been one at
the head of the list of extravagance – in an article relating
an incident at Drury Lane Theatre is the following – 'A
large piece of timber fell on Miss Poveys head & wounded

her severely she was of course incapable of performing
&c—who woud not of course believe Miss Poveys head
harder than a Statues after this
Sun. 2 Jan. Recievd a parcel from Mrs Emmerson took a
walk to 'Simons Wood' found 3 distinct species of the
'Bramble' or Mulberry – Henderson will have it there is
but 2 but I am certain he is wrong & believe there is 4 –
the common one that grows in the hedges – the larger sort
that grows on commons bearing larger fruit calld by
childern 'blackberry' the small creeping 'dewberry' that
runs along the ground in the land furrows & on the brinks
of brooks & a much larger one of the same kind growing
in woods botanists may say what they will for tho these are
all of a family they are distinctly different – there are 2
sorts of the wild rose the one in hedges bearing blush
colord flowers & the other much smaller in woods with
white ones
Wed. 5 Jan. Jiliflowers Polyanthuses Marigolds & the
yellow yarrow in flower & the double scarlet Anemonie
nearly out & crocuses peeping out above ground swelling
with flower the authoress (Miss Kent) of the 'Flora
Domestica'[86] says the snowdrop is the first spring flower
she is mistaken the yellow winter aconite is always earlier
& the first on the list of spring
Thur. 6 Jan. My dear boy Frederick is 1 year old this day
Fri. 7 Jan. Bought some cakes of colors with the intention
of trying to make sketches of curious snail horns Butterflys
Moths Sphinxes Wild flowers & whatever my wanderings
may meet with that are not too common
Sat. 8 Jan. A ryhming schoolmaster is the greatest bore in
literature the following ridicilous advertizement proves the
assertion taken from the 'Stamford Mercury'

Boston

Mr Gilberts boarding & day school will reopen on

Monday January 17th 1825

For favours past his heart must flow
& Kind regard to youth shall show

[57]

That Gilbert feels & grateful will
The noble art to learn instill

Sun. 9 Jan.   Newspaper Miracles Wonders Curiositys &c
&c under these heads I shall insert anything I can find
worth reading & laughing at – 'two extraordinary large eels
were last week taken upon the Saltings at Steeple in Dengre
hundred Essex – these monsters of their species (& there is
every reason to believe them to be the freshwater silver eel)
– one was seven feet in length twenty-one inches in
surcumferance & weighd fifty-seven pounds the other was
six feet long larger round then the former & weighd sixty-
two pound – twenty years back one was taken nearly six
feet long close to Portman marsh wall – in Essex a quarter
of a mile from Maldon bridge – a part of one of [the] eels
was eaten by our correspondent who speaks highly of its
flavor' – Essex herald A parish clerk 115 years old is now
able to read without spectacles & dig graves &c &c –
Stamford Mercury
Mon. 10 Jan.   Saw a whitethorn bush yesterday in Oxey
wood in the leaf all over & by next Sunday no doubt the
knots of may may be seen – the winter ackonite just
peeping out with its yellow flowers – the aron [arum] just
appearing under the hedges as in April & the Avens (a
common hedgerow plant) has never lost its leaves but
appears as green as at Spring
Tues. 11 Jan.   Began to fetch maiden earth from molehills
for my flower beds – heard the Mavis thrush sing for the
first time this winter it often sings earlier & has been heard
on Christmas day when the weather has been open
Thur. 13 Jan.   Helpd Billings to take in Beans
Fri. 14 Jan.   A scarlet daisey in flower in the Garden –
Receivd a latter from C. A. Elton who tells me there is a
many plants & ferns about Bristol downs & valleys &
'some rathe[r] peculiar to the country' I hope I shall be
able to go in Spring
Sat. 15 Jan.   This day is my Fathers birthday who is 60
years old – 'Thus runs the world away'
Sun. 16 Jan.   Took a walk in 'Porters snow close' to hunt
ferns in the morning & in Turnills 'heath wood' in the

afternoon found nothing but the fox fern which is the commonest of all about here – Receivd a letter from Mrs Emmerson & answerd it

Wed. 19 Jan. A slight storm of snow for the first time this winter – just compleated the 9th Chapter of my Life – corrected the poem on the 'Vanitys of the World' which I have written in imitation of the old poets on whom I mean to father it & send it to Montgomerys paper the 'Iris' or the 'Literary Chronicle' under that character

Thur. 20 Jan. Wrote a letter to Hessey

Fri. 21 Jan. 1825 A robin whistling on the plumb trees by the window I never heard one so early before

Sat. 22 Jan. 'A new Vegetable called the 'Asparagus Potatoe' has been introduced into this country it comes into season just as the asparagus goes out' – 'So little wind prevails in Italy that not a windmill is to be seen in any part of it, there were two in Venice but were taken down as usless for want of wind' – 'An elm tree suppos'd to be a thousand years old was blown down near Ludlow castle' – 'A blackbirds nest with four young ones was found a few days ago in Yorkshire' – Stamford Mercury

Sun. 23 Jan. Newspaper wonders 'There is now living at Barton an old lady of the name of Faunt who has nearly attained the great age of 105 years – she has lately cut *new teeth* to the great supprise of the family' – Stamford Mercury – took a walk in hilly wood brought home another plant of the white maidenhair fern that grows on a sallow stoven in a sort of spring wrote to Mr Sharp[87] of the dead letter office – finishd my 'two ballads to Mary' which I intend to send to the Literary Gazette as also my 3 sonnets to Bloomfield & I am weary of writing [two lines indecipherably scored out]

Tues. 25 Jan. A fine day the bees were out busily flying as if seeking flowers the sky was hung with light flying clouds & the season appeard as if the beginning of April

Wed. 26 Jan. Fetchd some soil from Cowper green for my ferns & flowers – the sharpest frost for this winter which woud not bare a boy to slide on – from what cause sprung the superstition of making No. 3 a fatal No? – it is so much so – that ghosts use it & never pay a visit without giving their (fashionable) signal of 3 raps to announce their arrival

Thur. 27 Jan. Recievd a letter from Mr Sharp & one from Lord Radstock – & answerd his Lordships sending in it the 'Vanitys of Life' a poem[88] – heard the buzz of the black beetle or cockchaffer[89] that flyes about in the autumn evenings & early in spring it is different to the brown or summer beetle which is described by Collins[90]

> the beetle winds
> His small but sullen horn

& is not so common

Sun. 30 Jan. Recievd a letter from Mrs Emmerson & a 'Litterary Gazette' from somebody in which is a Review of an unsuccessful attempt to reach Repulse Bay &c By Captain Lyon from which the following curious incident is extracted speaking of some graves of the Esquimaux he says 'Near the large grave was a third pile of stones covering the body of a child which was coiled up in the same manner. A snow bunting had found its way thro the loose stones which composed this little tomb & its now forsaken neatly built nest was found placed on the neck of the Child. As the Snow bunting has all the domestic Virtues of our English Redbreast it has always been considerd by us as the Robin of these dreary wilds & its lively chirp & fearless confidence have renderd it respected by the most hungry sportsmen – I could not on this occasion view its little nest placed on the breast of Infancy without wishing that I possesd the power of poetically expressing the feelings it excited'

Mon. 31 Jan. Went to Simons Wood for a succor of the Barberry bush to set in my Garden – saw the Corn[91] tree putting out into leaf – a yellow crocus & a bunch of single snowdrops in full flower – the mavis thrush has been singing all day long Spring seems begun – The woodbines all over the wood are in full leaf

Tues. 1 Feb. 1825 A beautiful morning took a walk in the fields saw some birch poles on the quick fencing & fancyd the bark of birch might make a good substitute for Paper it is easily parted in thin lairs & one shred of bark round the

tree woud split into 10 or a dozen sheets – I have tryd it &
find it recieves the ink very readily

Wed. 2 Feb. Went to walk in the fields & heard Ufford
bells chiming for a funeral when I enquird I found it was
for poor old John Cue of Ufford a friend of mine with
whom I workd some seasons at turnip hoeing for which he
was famous – he knew my Grandfather well & told me
many reccolections of their young day follys – John Cue
was once head Gardener for Lord Manners of Ufford hall –
he was fond of flowers & books & possessed a many
curious ones of the latter among which was 'Parkinson'[92]

Thur. 3 Feb. Recievd a letter from Hessey with £5
enclosed & a parcel containing 2 Nos of the new series of
London Mag; and 'Waladmor'[93] a German-Scotch novel – if
Job was living now he woud stand a chance to gain his
wish 'O that mine enemy woud write a book' for this is
the age of book making – & like the smallpox almost
everybody catches the plague

Fri. 4 Feb. The first winters day a sharp frost & a night
fall of snow drifting in heaps by a keen wind – there has
been a deal of talk about the forwardness of this season –
but last season was not much behind – on the third of this
month I found an hedge-sparrows nest in Billings Boxtrees
before the window with three eggs in it I lookd again in
March & found two young ones pen-featherd starved to
death – she laid again in the same nest & brought off a
fledgd brood in April

Sat. 5 Feb. Severe frost – Recieved a joint letter from
Lord Radstock & Mrs Emmerson under a Frank which was
put into post too soon for which a charge of 1 py was
made – 'Knaves in office' watch chances as the cat watches
mice & are of that species of animal that catch their prey
by supprise

Sun. 6 Feb. Recieved a letter from Mrs Gilchrist – heard
by Ned Simpson of Stamford that a bird of the hawk kind
was shot at a fountain in hollywell Park of a large size
which he calls the 'hair legd falcon' Heard by the same of a
white mole being caught in Stamford field

Thur. 10 Feb. Fine day the bees are out & busily seeking
for wax among the little flowers of the yellow acconite – a

sparrow is building its nest in a hole in the old wallnut tree in the Taylors garden

Fri. 11 Feb. Saw the first young Lamb this season – saw a blue violet on the Ivy bank next the lane in Billings Close

Sat. 12 Feb. Recieved a letter from Vandyke in which he appears as the Editor of my Poems they chuse who they please this time but my choice comes next & I think I shall feel able to do it myself he wishes me to alter the title of my song written in imitation of Peggy Band to Peggy Bland because the old ballad is bad I did it in memory of the music & shall not alter it

Sun. 13 Feb. Recieved a letter from Dr. Darling – An odd sort of fellow came today with a bag full of old school summing books wanting me to buy them & vowing he was the author of them & that I might make a good bargain by publishing them what odd characters there are in the world the fellow fancied that I was excessive ignorant to palm such ignorant impudence upon me for truth after he found that his scheme woud not take he begd two pence & departed – he is the son of an odd fellow at Baston he is a little foolish in his nature & they put him a long while to school to compleat what she began –

my dear Anna taken very ill

Mon. 14 Feb. Wrote to Vandyk & Dr Darling in my letter to Vandyk I inserted the tune of 'Peggy Band' There is a many beautiful tunes to these provincial Ballads such is the 'White Cockade' 'Wars Alarms' 'Down the Burn Davy' old & new 'Thro the wood laddy' 'Dusty Miller' 'Highland Laddie' & a very beautiful one I forget the title it begins 'A witherd old gipsey one day I espied Who bade me shun the thick woods & said something beside' but the old woman that sung it is gone – the 'Old Guardian Angels' 'Banks of Banna' & a thousand others

Tues. 15 Feb. Heard the Blackbird sing in Hillywood – recievd a Valentine from Mrs Emmerson [three lines inked out] my Anna is somthing better

Wed. 16 Feb. Heard the Skylark sing at Swordy well – saw a piece of bayonet & gun barrel found while digging a stone pit this proves the story that superstition tells of a battle fought here by the rebels in Cromwells time – it is

said were there is smoke there is fire & I often think were
superstition lingers with her storys there is always some
truth in them – brought home a bush of Ling or heath to
plant in the garden

Thur. 17 Feb.   Saw a large bunch of blue violets in flower
& a root of the Bedlam Cowslip

Sat. 19 Feb.   Recieved a Newspaper from Montgomery[94] in
which my poem of the 'Vanitys of Life' was inserted with
an ingenius & flattering comment past upon it praise from
such a person as Montgomery is heart stirring & its the
only one from a poet that I have met with – went to
Turnills Heath close to get some furze bushes to set in the
Garden

Sun. 20 Feb.   Found several pieces of roman pot in
Harrisons top close on the hill over which the road crosses
to the Tindhills at the north-east corner of Oxey wood one
piece was the letterd & Artis says they are Roman & I
verily believe some Roman camp or pottery was made there

Mon. 21 Feb.   A robin busy at building its nest in the
Garden

Tues. 22 Feb.   A hedge Sparrow building its nest in one of
Billingss Box trees

Sat. 26 Feb.   Recieved a Letter from Lord Radstock filld
with scraps of Newspaper Poetry among which was a
pretty valentine by Montgomery & some verses said to be
written by Lord Byron they are in his manner – the rest
after perusal of the Newspapers are 'nothings' – When his
Lordship sees anything he fancys better then the rest he
always attributes it to Mrs Emmerson or some of his
friends as he has done now one to her & one to Vandyke

Sun. 27 Feb.   Recieved a letter in ryhme from a John
Pooley – a very dull fooley [two lines inked out] who ran
me 10d further in debt as I had not money to pay the
postage

Tues. 1 Mar. 1825   Saw today the largest piece of Ivy I
ever saw in my life mailing a tree which it nearly surpassd
in size in Oxey Wood it was thicker then my thigh & its
cramping embraces seemd to diminish the tree to a dwarf –
it has been asserted by some that Ivy is very injurious to
trees & by others that it does no injury at all – I cannot

[63]

decide against it – the large pieces were covered all over
with root-like fibres as thick as hair & they represented the
limbs of animals more then the bark of a tree

Wed. 2 Mar. Found a Mavis Thrushes[95] nest with 3 eggs
these birds always build early they make a nest like a
blackbirds but instinct has taught them a lesson against the
cold which the other has no occasion for & that is they
never line their nests without wool which keeps the nest
warm at this early season they always begin to sing as soon
as the male blossoms of the hazel or (Trails) make their
appearance & build their nests when female flowers put
forth their little crimson threads at the end of the buds to
recieve the impregning dust of the male dangling trails

Thur. 3 Mar. This is Pattys Birthday

Fri. 4 Mar. Went to Ailsworth heath to fetch ling or
common heath & furze bushes to set in my garden – went
in Bates spinney to hunt the black maiden hair found none
but saw some of the largest furze & common brakes I had
ever seen my friend Billings measured a furze bush which
was 11 foot & a ½ high & a brake branch 9 foot & a ¼
found a curious sort of Iris or flag growing in a pond in
the wood & fancy it not a common one brought a bit
home to set

Sat. 5 Mar. Recieved a letter from Lord Radstock & Mrs
Emmerson also one from a Mr Weston[96] the Editor of poor
Bloomfields Letters & Remains requesting me to send him
the letters I have of the poet & asking permission to
publish those of mine poor Bloomfield I wish that death
had left me a little longer the pleasures of his friendship –
Went to see the fox cover on Etton field sown with furze
some years ago which now present a novel appearance &
thrive better than on their native heath tho the place is low
ground

Sun. 6 Mar. Recieved a parcel from Hessey with the
Magazine & a leaf of the new poems also a present of Miss
Kents Sylvan Sketches[97] she seems to be a thorough book
maker [two lines inked out] Parish Officers are modern
Savages as the following fact will testifye: Crowland Abbey
– 'certain surveyors have lately dug up several foundation
stones of the Abbey & also a great quantity of stone coffins

for the purpose of repairing the parish roads' – Stamford
Mercury – Anna taken agen for the worse yesterday had a
terrible fever all night & remains in a doubtful state –
Mon. 7 Mar.   Wrote to E. T. Artis – Mrs Gilchrist & Mrs
Emmerson – enclosing one in Artis's Letter (to get it
Franked) for Mrs W. Wright of Clapham – requesting her
to give me a bulb of the 'Tyger lily' & a sucker of the
'White Province Rose'
Tues. 8 Mar.   Wrote to Hessey & to Jos Weston of 12
Providence Row Finsbury Square London enclosing my
letters of Bloomfield for his use in a forthcoming vol of his
Correspondence – went to Royce Wood to get some
Service trees to set in Billings close
Wed. 9 Mar.   I had a very odd dream last night & I take it
as an ill omen for I dont expect that the book will meet a
better fate – I thought I had one of the proofs of the new
poems from London & after looking at it awhile it shrank
thro my hands like sand & crumbled into dust—the birds
were singing in Oxey Wood at 6 o clock this evening as
loud & various as at May
Thur. 10 Mar.   Heard an Anecdote yesterday of Dr
Dodd[98] which is well known & considerd authentic among
the common people it is said that Dr Dodd was taunted on
his way to the place of execution by a lady who had envied
his popularity & looking out of a window as he passd she
exclaimed 'Now Dr Dodd weres your God' when he bade
her look in the last chapter of Micah & read the 8th 9th &
10th verses[99] for an answer which she did & dyd soon
afterwards of a broken heart
Fri. 11 Mar.   Intend to call my Natural History of
Helpstone 'Biographys of Birds & Flowers' with an
appendix on Animals & Insects[100] – The frogs have began
to croke & spawn in the ponds & dykes
Sat. 12 Mar.   Recieved the first Proof of the Shepherds
Calendar from Hessey to correct – & a letter from Lord
Radstock in which he seems to be offended at a late
opinion of mine of some Newspaper Poems that he sent me
as specimens of the beautiful – & he thanks his stars that
his taste is not so refined as to make him above admiring
them – The word refinement has lost its original use & is

nothing more then a substitute for fashionable coquette which I thank my stars for keeping me too ignorant to learn

Sun. 13 Mar. Recieved a letter from the Editor of Bloomfields Correspondence enclosing the return of my letter of Bloomfield & a scrap of his handwriting written in his summer house at Shefford an Inscription in it which I hear is now defaced what a sad thing it is to see the relics of such poets destroyed who woud not have made a pilgrimage to have seen the summer house & its inscription as left by the Bard – in the same letter also was a pretty unaffected letter from Hannah Bloomfield his daughter she seems to inherit the gentle unassuming manners of feelings for which her father was loved & esteemed – lent Henderson 3 Nos. of the New London Mag: & Review[101] took a walk to Open Copy to see the Nutt trees in flower which promise a great nutting season

Mon. 14 Mar. My double Scarlet Anemonie in full flower – A sharp frosty morning

Tues. 15 Mar. I have been reading over Mrs Barbaulds Lessons for Childern[102] to my eldest child who is continually teasing me to read them I find by this that they are particularly suited to the tastes of childern as she is never desirous of hearing anything read a second time but them

Wed. 16 Mar. Took a walk to hunt pootys about Royce Close & the Tindhills – went to visit an old favourite spot in Oxey Wood that used to be smotherd with Ferns – got some sallow trees to set in Billings close & a stoven of Black alder to set in my garden

Thur. 17 Mar. Recieved a letter & present of Books from Lord Radstock containing Hannah Moores 'Spirit of Prayer'[103] – Bp Wilsons 'Maxims'[104] Burnets 'Life of God in the Soul of Man'[105] – 'A New Manual of Prayer' & Watsons 'Answer to Paine'[106] a quiet unaffected defence of the Bible & an example for all controversialists to go bye w[h]ere railing has no substitute for argument – I have not read Tom Paine but I have always understood him to be a low blackguard

Fri. 18 Mar. The sharp frosty mornings still continue

Sat. 19 Mar.   Had from Drakards a folio blank book price 9s–d to insert the best of my poems in that Hessey says he will send down

Sun. 20 Mar.   Still sharp frosty mornings – Recieved a letter from Mrs Emmerson with an Ode to Spring – Spring is a wonderful mother for ryhmes

Mon. 21 Mar.   Had a double Polanthus & single white Hepatica sent me from Stamford round which was rapped a curious prospectus of an 'Everyday Book' by W. Hone.[107] If such a thing was well got up it woud make one of the most entertaining things ever published & – I think the prospectus bids fair to do something there is a fine quotation from Herrick for a Motto how delightful is the freshness of these old poets it is meeting with green spots in deserts

Tues 22 Mar.   A cold wintry day

Wed. 23 Mar.   Recieved a parcel from Holbeach with a Letter & the Scientific Receptacle[108] from J. Savage – they have inserted my poems & have been lavish with branding every corner with 'J. Clares' – How absurd are the serious meant images or attempts at fine writing in these young writers one of them concludes a theme on a dead schoolmaster with a very pathetic & sublime wish as he fancys perhaps 'wishing that the tear he leaves on his grave may grow up a marble monument to his memory' – This is the first crop of tears I have ever heard of sown with an intention to grow

Thur. 24 Mar.   Recievd a letter from Lord Radstock with a packet of Newspapers from Mrs Emmerson

Sun. 27 Mar.   This is Palm Sunday – I went to the woods to seek some branches of the sallow palms for the childer calld by them 'geese & goslings' & 'Cats & Kittens' – Susan Simpson & her brother came to see me – lent her the 2 Vols of Walladmor[109]

Wed. 30 Mar.   Recieved a letter from Vandyk which proves all my suspicions are well founded I suspected that he had not seen those M.S.S. which I considered my best poems & he says in his letter that he has not [4 lines scored out & undecipherable]

Thur. 31 Mar.   Artis & Henderson came to see me & we

[67]

went to see the Roman Station agen Oxey wood which he
says is plainly roman – he told me that he went three times
& sent oftener for the M.S.S. which they did not send at
last – [3 lines scored out & undecipherable]
Fri. 1 April 1825   My Sister Sophy is 27 year old today
Recieved from Wilson Vyse's 'Tutor's Guide' 2 Vols[110]
Sat. 2 April   'The Lingfield & Crowhurst choir sung
several select pieces from Handel in the Cavity of a Yew
tree in the church yard of the latter place The tree is 36 feet
in Circumference & is now in a growing state – The hollow
was filled up like a room & sufficiently large to contain the
performers – On cleaning out the interior of the tree some
years since a 7lb cannon ball was discovered which no
doubt had been fired into it; it was cut out from the solid
part of the tree –' Stamford Mercury
Sun. 3 April   Two gentlemen came to see me from Milton
one of them appeard to be a sensible & well informed man
he talkd much of the poets but did not like Wordsworth &
when I told him I did he instantly asked me wether I did
not like Byron better I don't like these comparisons to
knock your opinions on the head with – I told him that I
read Wordsworth oftener then I did Byron & he seemd to
express his supprise at it by observing that he coud not
read Wordsworth at all
Fri. 8 April   Recieved a letter from Lord Radstock & one
from Mrs Emmerson with an offer that Mr Clutterbuck the
Attorney will draw up my will if I chuse which
oppertunity I shall certainly take hold of
Sun. 10 April   Found a branch of whitethorn in Porters
Snow close knotted & nearly in flower it is considerd very
early if a branch of May as it is calld can be found on the
first of new May
Wed. 13 April   The blackthorn showing flower
Thur. 14 April   My mother is 67 years old this day she has
been afflicted with a dropsy for this 20 years & has for all
that outlived a large family of brothers & sisters & remains
'the last of the flock' the Snakehead or frittillary[111] in
flower also the light-blue pink & white Hyacinths –
Bluebell or Harebell in flower the Primrose Violet &
Bedlam Cowslips fading out of flower

[68]

Fri. 15 April   Recieved a letter from Lord Radstock in which his Lordship says that Vandyk is going out of town for a while this is the man that was to get my new book thro the press in 6 weeks & with the assistance of Taylor & Hessey has been a month about one proof of it [2 lines scored out and indecipherable]

Sat. 16 April   Took a walk in the field a birds nesting & botanizing & had like to have been taken up as a poacher in Hillywood by a meddlesome consieted keeper belonging to Sir John Trollop he swore that he had seen me in act more than once of shooting game when I never shot even so much as a sparrow in my life – what terrifying rascals these woodkeepers & gamekeepers are they make a prison of the forrests & are its gaolers

Sun. 17 April   I have waited 3 weeks for a new proof of the Shepherds Calendar & nothing has come which was to be in 3 days – I have sent for some rough copys of Poems which I sent up to Taylor when the 'Village Minstrel' was in the press & I have not got them yet & never shall I expect – I want them to finish some for a future publication & correct others – [4 lines scored out and undecipherable] I have never as yet had a settling – Recieved a letter from Dr Darling – no proofs yet – saw a solitary Fieldfare in Oxey wood I never observed one so late before – wrote to Hessey in a manner that I am always very loath to write but I coud keep my patience no longer

Mon. 18 April   Resumed my letters on Natural History in good earnest & intend to get them finished with this year if I can get out into the fields for I will insert nothing but what comes or has come under my notice

Tues. 19 April   The Swallows have made their appearance I saw one today & I heard by a cowboy that they were come three days ago

Wed. 20 April   Recieved a letter from Taylor in answer to mine to Hessey of last Sunday – He is very pettish respecting my anxiety & irritation & says that if my friends who gave me the advice & cautions &c respecting the neglect & mystery of booksellers or myself can find a Publisher who can do better by them then he does he will readily return the M.S.S. – but he throws a river in the

[69]

way for me to cross by saying that tho none of their
distrust can do no good it may do harm – now if it can do
harm to find fault with actions that deserve no
commendation I am sure it can do no good to speak in
their praise

Thur. 21 April   Heard the Nightingale for the first time
this season in Royce wood

Fri. 22 April   Went to Milton – Saw the red headed brown
linnet[112] smaller than the brown do – saw a Pettichap or
hoverbird[113] – & a large flock of Fieldfares – brought home
a white Primrose heard a many Nightingales – in the
evening I heard a bird make a long continued noise for a
minute together like a childs skreeker or a cricket but much
louder[114] – Henderson promises to give me some
information respecting the birds about Milton

Sat. 23 April   Saw the redstart or Firetail today & little
Willow wren – the blackthorn tree in full flower that shines
about the hedges like cloaths hung out to dry – Saw in the
Stamford paper that the lost leaf of Domesday book was
found & had no time to Copy out the account

Sun. 24 April   No Proofs of the New Poems yet –
Recieved a Letter from Lord Radstock & Mrs Emmerson

Mon. 25 April   Heard a terrible kick-up with the Rats in
the ceiling last night & might have made up a tollerable
faith to believe them ghosts – A thunderstorm several claps
very loud in the distance came from south west

Tues. 26 April   This used to be 'Breakday' when the Fen
commons used to be broke as it was calld by turning in the
stock it used to be a day of busy note with the villages but
Enclosure has spoiled all

Wed. 27 April   Heard the Cuckoo for the first time this
Season – it was said to be heard a week back by a Shepherd
– Saw the large Grey Wagtail I think it a bird of passage[115]
as I have never seen it in winter – some young Plants of
Ash & Maple showing leaf – Saw a bird with a dark line
over each ear I think it one of the fly catchers

Thur. 28 April   Hedge-Sparrow finished her nest in
Billings Box-tree & laid one egg—Wallnutt showing leaf –
Sycamore & Horse chesnutt nearly coverd—I observed a
Snail on his journey at full speed & I marked by my watch

that he went 13 Inches in 3 minutes which was the utmost he coud do without stopping to wind or rest It was the large Garden snail

Fri. 29 April The hedge Sparrow in the Box tree has spent about 12 days building her nest the Robin in the wall about 14 & the Jenny-wren near 3 weeks heard all this last night the sort of watch ticking noise calld a death watch I observed there was one on each side the chamber & as soon as one ceased ticking the other began I think it is a call that the male & female use in the time of cohabiting the jenny wrens nest with the outside just built I mean to see how long she is about the lining

Sat. 30 April Recieved another letter from the editor of Bloomfields Correspondence requesting me to alter a line in my sonnets on Bloomfield 'Thy injured muse & memory need no sigh' & asking permission to publish only two of them which I shall not agree with either way Editors are troubled with nice amendings & if Doctors were as fond of amputation as they are of altering & correcting the world woud have nothing but cripples

Sun. 1 May 1825 A Salmon *near* 20 lbs weight was caught about a fortnight ago by Robt Nassau Sutton Esq while trolling in the river Trent near Kelham Hall – Stamford Mercury

Mon. 2 May Bradfords Club feast next door never went into the Yard to see them a thing I never did in my life before – illness makes the merriest pastimes of life as tiresome fooleries & turns the sweetest offerings of pleasure to gall –

Tues. 3 May Wrote a letter to Taylor[116] & one to Mrs Emmerson

Fri. 6 May Could not sleep all night got up at three o clock in the morning & walkd about the fields – the birds were high in their songs in Royce Wood & almost deafening I heard the Cricket bird[117] again in full cry in Royce Wood it is just like a childs screeker – saw a Hawk-like bird[118] that made an odd noise like one of the notes of the Nightingale as if to decoy his prey in sight

Sat. 7 May Sent some Pootys & Ferns to Henderson yesterday

Sun. 8 May   Went to Walk in the fields saw the white
thorn in some places about the hedges covered over with
May & the Wilding or Crab also was smothered with
blossom the Maple was in full flower

Mon. 9 May   Wrote another portion of my Life & took a
Walk to seek a Nightingales nest – found a Song thrushes
in bushy close by the side of a young oak with 4 eggs
never saw one of this kind in such a place before

Tues. 10 May   Saw a male & female of the Tree sparrow
(as I supposed them) in Royce close hedge next the lane the
cock bird had a very black head & its shades of brown
were more deep & distinct then the house sparrow the
female when flying showd two white feathers in her tail
they seemd to have a nest in the hedgerow but I coud not
find it – saw a Pettichap in Bushy close its note is more
like 'Chippichap'¹¹⁹ it keeps in continual motion on the
tops of trees uttering its note

Wed. 11 May   Recieved a letter last night from Henderson
with a plant of the Double Marsh marigold – the male
flowers of the Wallnutt ripe & falling off

Thur. 12 May   It is often reported that the Sky lark never
sings but on the Wing this report is worth little truth like a
many others I saw one this morning sing on the ground

Fri. 13 May   Met with an extrordinary incident today
while walking in Open wood to hunt a Nightingales nest –
I popt unawares on an old Fox & her four young Cubs
that were playing about – she saw me & instantly
approachd me growling like an angry dog I had no stick &
tryd all I coud to fright her by imitating the bark of a
foxhound which only irritated her the more & if I had not
retreated a few paces back she woud have seized me when I
set up an haloo she started

Sat. 14 May   Recieved the April & May Magazine from
London with a letter from Hessey & one from Vandyke
that has lain ever since 15th of March the Magazine is very
dull a Note also from Miss Kent accompanied the parcel to
request my assistance to give her information for her
intended History of Birds¹²⁰ but if my assistance is not
worth more than 12 lines it is worth nothing & I shall not
interfere

[72]

Sun. 15 May Extracts from the Stamford Mercury 'Coals were first used in England in the reign of Edward the 1st the smoke was supposed to corrupt the air so much that he forbad the use of them'–
'A fellow who passes himself off on the ignorant as a prophet is extorting money from the ignorant by telling them that a flying serpent will come to destroy them against whose venom he sells spells that will ensure their safety –' The delusion respecting the flying serpent still continues: The fatal days were stated to be thursday last the 18th & 28th The Prophet has been travelling thro Dorset & the adjoining counties offering his charms for sale – has not found a deficiency of dupes yet of those who demur he asks 'If you will not receive the servant how will you receive the master when he comes'

Tues. 17 May At a meeting of Florists held at the old Kings Head at Newark last week prizes were adjudged as follows:

Auriculas

First	Grimes Privateer	—	Mr Ordoyne
Second	Stretches Alexander	—	Mr Ordoyne
Third	Wild's Black & Clear	—	Mr Welby

Polyanthus

First	Twineys Princess of Wales	—	Mr Ordoyne
Second	Trillinghams Tantararia	—	Mr Taylor
Third	England's Defiance	—	Mr Clark

Sun. 22 May Newspaper Odditys

'A spirited London bookseller announces that he is printing the Duke of Yorks Speech against the Catholics in *letters of gold* – This is shining fame at least – 'The total population of America is 34,280,000 of which 11,287,000 are Protestants 22,177,000 Roman Catholics & 820,000 Indians not Christians' 'At Wieland in Poland the imagination is confounded at the idea of finding after a descent of 850 steps in the salt mines vast Halls (The Hall of Klosky is 360 feet high & 180 feet wide) stabling for 80 horses storehouses offices for Clerks & three Chappels the whole of the fittings altars crucifixes tables desks & seats worked in salt!' Stamford Mercury – Recieved a letter from Lord

Radstock with one enclosed of a Mr Boilau with a flattering compliment on my poems calling me a pretty flower

Mon. 23 May   More Wonders from the Mercury 'A Clergyman of the established Church name Benson now attracts larger congregations at St Giles' church then the celebrated Mr Irving[121] once did at the Caledonian Mr Benson's Chief Characteriztic is calm & dignified reasoning Mr Irving's powerful eloquence & vehement action' '211 Stage Coaches pass weekly through Daventry Northamptonshire' – Stamford Mercury

Tues. 24 May   The Catholics have lost their bill once more & its nothing but right they shoud when one beholds the following sacred humbugs which their religion hurds up & sanctifys – 'A list of Catholic relics in a church at Dobberau a village in Mecklenburg' – From Nugent's Travels[122] – A small quantity of flax which the Virgin Mary had for spinning – A bundle of hay which the three wise men of the east had for their cattle & left behind them at bethlehem – a bone of Ignatius Loyola the founder of the Jesuits – A piece of poor Lazaruses Garment – a bone of St Christopher & first joint of his thumb – a piece of linnen cloth which the Virgin Mary wove with her own hands – a piece of the head belonging to the fish mentioned in Tobit – The napkin which the bridegroom made use of at the marriage of Cana in Galilee – a hair of St. Jerome's Mustachios – Part of Judas bowels which gushed out as he burst asunder – the sissars with which Delila cut off Sampson's hair – a piece of the apron which the butcher wore when he killed the calf upon the return of the prodigal son – one of the five smooth stones which David put into his bag when he went to encounter the giant Goliah – a branch of the tree on which Absalom hung by the hair – The Deeds of St Thomas as the Apostle of St Paul & of St Peter – A piece of St Peters fishing net – the Priest told the traveller that one of the relics had been stolen in the last Century & it was no less than a quill of the Angel Gabriels Wing

Thur. 26 May   Took up my Hyacinth bulbs & laid them in ridges of earth to dry – made a new frame for my

[74]

Ariculas – found a large white orchis in Oxey Wood of a curious species & very rare[123] I watched a Bluecap or Blue Titmouse feeding her young whose nest was in a wall close to an Orchard she got caterpillars out of the Blossoms of the apple trees & leaves of the plumb – she fetched 120 Caterpillars in half an hour – now supposing she only feeds them 4 times a day a quarter of an hour each time she fetches in no less than 480 Caterpillars & I shoud think treble that number

Fri. 27 May Recieved a letter & a packet of Newspapers yesterday from Mrs Emmerson in which she promises to send me some Polyanthuses from Bath & Carnations also –

Sat. 28 May Found the old Frog in my garden that has been there this four years I know it by a mark which it recieved from my spade 4 years ago I thought it woud dye of the wound so I turnd it up on a bed of flowers at the end of the garden which is thickly covered with ferns & bluebells & am glad to see it has recoverd – In Winter it gets into some straw in a corner of the garden & never ventures out till the beginning of May when it hides among the flowers & keeps its old bed never venturing further up the garden –

Sun. 29 May The following Advertisement is from the Observer of Sunday May 22 1825 'Just published The Speech of his Royal Highness the Duke of York in the House of Lords the 25 April 1825 Printed by J. Whittaker (with the same splendour as the account of the Coronation of his Majesty) in letters of Gold on the finest Card paper price 10/6 Sold by Septimus Prowett 23 Old Bond Street' Well done Septimus Prowett the speech is an open & honest one & well deserves it – Heard the most severe thunderclap yesterday that I ever heard in my life it was heard instantly (only 3 pulses) after the flash – Found a very scarce & curious orchis[124] of an iron grey color or rather a pale rusty tinge with a root like the pilewort I cannot make out its name – I found last week a fine white piegon orchis[125] which is seldom found

Mon. 30 May Took a Walk yesterday to Bassetts close at the bottom of the wormstalls to see the Ash tree that the lightning struck on Saturday it took off the large top &

splinterd the body to atoms driving large pieces of it in all
directions round the tree to the distance of fifty yards the
stump of the trunk left standing was pilled of the bark all
round & split to the bottom I never saw such terrible
power of lightning in my life before: people came to see it
from all the neighbouring villages & took away the
fragments as curiositys

Tues. 31 May   My dear Child Eliza was taken ill of a fever
on Sunday night & is as yet no better – Sent a letter &
parcel to Mrs Emmerson with the 'Parish' & my new Will
for Mr Clutterbuck to draw up Mrs Bellairs of Woodcroft
Castle came to see my garden – Artis told me he fancied
that the place in Harrisons close was a Roman Pottery I
have since reccolected that there used to be a large hole
about two stones throw from it called 'Potters Hole' when
I was a boy & filled up since the Enclosure this may go far
for his opinion

Thur. 2 June 1825   This is my darling Annas Birthday
who is 5 years old a weakling flower fast fading in the bud
– withering untimelessly – Recieved a parcel from Hessey
with the Mag: & the first proof agen corrected for good
with a note from Hessey & a long letter from Taylor very
kindly worded in which he speaks of dissolving partnership
with Hessey on Midsummer next

Fri. 3 June   Finishd planting my Ariculas – went a-
Botanizing after Ferns & Orchises & caught a cold in the
wet grass which has made me as bad as ever – got the tune
of 'Highland Mary' from Wisdom Smith a gipsey &
pricked another sweet tune without name as he fiddled it

Sat. 4 June   Saw 3 fellows at the end of Royce Wood
who I found were laying out the plan for an 'Iron railway'
from Manchester to London – it is to cross over Round
Oak Spring by Royce Wood Corner for Woodcroft Castle
I little thought that fresh intrusions woud interrupt & spoil
my solitudes after the Enclosure they will despoil a boggy
place that is famous for Orchises at Royce Wood end

Sun. 5 June   Returned the proof to Hessey wrote a note to
Hessey & one to Mrs Wright of Clapham accompanied
with some flowers viz – 'Lilies of the Valley' 'Shepherds
Goldilocks' 'Jerusalem Cowslips' 'Yellow flowerd Yarrow'

'Lilac flowerd Cranesbill' 'Black flowerd Cranesbill' &
'Pencil flowered Do'. – Read a continuation of a good
paper in the London on 'A poor Students struggles thro
Cambridge &c' the rest are moderates among the
middlings[126]

Mon. 6 June   Went to see Mrs Bellairs garden at
Woodcroft with Anna saw a Scarlet Anemonie & White
Peony both very handsome the Mote round the Garden has
a very fine effect & the long Bridges that cross it made of
planks & railed with crooked pieces of oak I thought of the
time of Cromwell while walking about it & felt the
difference – Swallows had several nests under the bridge

Tues. 7 June   Recieved another parcel from Hessey with
another proof of the Poems Viz the 'Sorrows of Love'[127]
Taylor has cut out a good deal & some things which I
think might have stood the parcel also brought a present of
Aytons Essays[128] a young writer of great promise which
was killed in the bud these Essays are exelent & contain a
great deal more of the Human Heart than an affectedly
written book with that Title

Wed. 8 June   Poor old Coz Day the Mole Catcher dyed
tonight after a short illness – he has been a tenant of the
meadows & fields for half a Century

Thur. 9 June   Recieved a letter from Mrs Emmerson &
wrote an answer to it – Returned the proofs of January &
the Broken Heart & wrote to Taylor – sent some flowers
to Mrs Bellairs & am promised the 'Scarlet Anemonie'
'White Peony' & 'Pink Brompton Stocks'

Fri. 10 June   Saw the blue-grey or lead-colored Flycatcher
for the first time this season they are called 'Egypt Birds'
by the common people from their note which seems to
resemble the sound of the word 'Egypt' they build in old
walls like the red start & Grey Wagtail

Mon. 13 June   My dear Eliza is 3 years old today – I feel
anxious to insert these memorandums of my affections as
Memory though a secondary is the soul of time & life the
principal but its shadow – Observed an Eclipse or some
other Phenomen of the Sun this Morning not noticed in the
Almanack I first saw it about half past four & it continued

till after five it had exactly the same appearance as an Eclipse & I believe it was nothing else

Sun. 19 June   Recievd a letter from Taylor in which he says that there is twice as much more as he wants for the Shepherds Calendar a few months back one of his causes for delay was that there was not enough to begin on nothing has made a wide difference here by time & left a puzzling Paradox behind it – which tells that he is a very dillatory chap – recieved a letter from Mrs Emmerson with a Parcel containing a present of a Waistcoat & some fine Polyanthus Brompton Stock & Geranium Seed

Tues. 21 June   Wrote a letter to Taylor – found a birds nest in the thatch of a hovel gable end in Billings yard think it a Flycatchers it resembles in color & shape something of the chat or White throat or more like the sedge bird then either the female sits hard & the cock feeds her with catterpillars from the leaves of trees

Thur. 23 June   Wrote to Mrs Emmerson & sent a letter to Hone Every Day book with a poem which I fatherd on Andrew Marvel[129]

Sat. 2 July 1825   Received a letter from Hessey with the Dividend or half yearly payment of the money in the funds & Lord Spencers Annuity – they always send it in written drafts to be drawn on their bankers for what reason I cannot tell unless it is to make a safe carrying I wanted £10 more than my sallarys but they have not sent it this time & have only sent me the £15 which belongs to me – Wrote to Mrs Emmerson & sent some verses in imitation of the old Poets to Hone's Every Day Book – 'On Death' – The Baloon with Mr Green & Miss Stocks passed over our garden opposite the wallnutt tree

Sun. 3 July   Today is Helpstone Feast Wrestling & fighting the ploughmans fame is still kept up with the usual determined spirit

Thur. 7 July   Wrote an answer to Hesseys letter of the 30th of June which contained a draft for my dividend & salary & enquired after the stoppage of the new poems also was forced to solicit them anew to send me £10 which I want to pay off my half yearly accounts

Sat. 9 July   Mr Sharp[130] from London called on me

[78]

Sun. 10 July   Recieved a letter from Hessey with the £10 which I wanted more then my Sallary came to – & with the News also that they have sold the London Mag:

Mon. 11 July   Started to Milton – a very pleasant morning saw a bird that was an entire stranger to me about the size & shape of a green linnet with wings of a brown grey color & the crown of the head a deep black that extended downward no further then the eyes it had an odd appearance & tho Artis looked thro Pennant he coud not find anything resembling it & believes it to be an unnoticed species of the linnet tribe[131]

Tues. 12 July   Went to day to see Artis found him busy over his antiquitys & Fossils he told me a curious thing about the manner in which the Golden crested wren builds her nest he says it is the only english bird that suspends its nest which it hangs on three twigs of the fir branch & it glews the eggs at the bottom of the nest with the gum out of the tree to keep them from being blown out by the wind which often turns them upside down without injury

Wed. 13 July   This day I am thirty-two (or thirty three I am not certain which)[132] – & my health was drank at Milton by two very pretty girls Mrs P—r & Mrs B—n who wishd I might treble the number but I did not drink it in return [3 lines scored out] Henderson has promised me a curious 'Everlasting Pea' a climbing Rose the Monkey Flower Feather Hyacinth & some Chrisanthemums

Thur. 14 July   Recieved a letter from Lord Radstock in which his Lordship has made another troublesome request for his letters which he has written to me I cannot hunt them up at present

Fri. 15 July   Recieved a letter from Mrs Emmerson in which she tells me that Rippingille is come up & she wants me to start tomorrow – this is one of the hottest days I have known & all my ferns is nearly scorchd up – Began to teach Eliza Holmes the common rules of Arithmetic at the restless request of her parents who are anxious for me to learn her

Sat. 16 July   Still uncommonly Hot

Thur. 21 July   Paid Stevenson for the Stamford Mercury & gave it up as too expensive

Sun. 24 July Found a species of Broom in Bushy Close of a dwarf kind the like sort grows in great quantitys on Casterton Cowpasture – the weather changed very cold but still dry

Mon. 25 July 'A hive of Bees natives of New South Wales has been recently brought to this country – The Bees are very small & have no Sting but their honey is peculiarly fine' – Stamford Mercury

Wed. 27 July Recieved the 28 No of the Every Day book in which is inserted a poem of mine which I sent under the assumed name of 'James Gilderoy' from Surfleet as being the production of Andrew Marvel & printed in the Miscellany of the Spalding Antiquarys – I shall venture agen under another name after a while – Viz. 'Poem on Death'

Fri. 29 July Recieved a proof from Taylor – the plan is again altered[133] & he now intends to print the Months only & leave out the Tales this plan is one that puts the worst first & leaves the best for a future oppertunity – this proof contains 'February' & 'April' – the last is good for nothing & is not worth troubling the printer with – the poem on Spring is the best in the bundle & woud supply its place well

Sat. 30 July Sharp came to bid me good bye before he started to London A young Lady was with him of very amiable & pleasing manners who was very fond of Poetry & flowers

Sun. 31 July Recieved a letter from Mrs Emmerson in which she has discovered me to be the Author of the Verses on Death in the every day book signed Marvel she has oftener been wrong in her guesses & I think if I had not given her some hints of it before I sent it she woud not have found it out now

Mon. 1 August 1825 Heard an old Fen Farmer say today that on his farm he finds a great deal of wood particularly Oak Hazel & Yew in the earth he says that the earth is actually nothing else but a decomposition of wood & that it will grow nothing but Oats he says that the Hazel will burn well as fire wood but the Oak dyes out unless continually blown – he also talked of great quantitys of shells being found as white as Dogs teeth

Tues. 2 Aug.   Wrote a Letter to William Hone's 'Every Day book' signed Roberts with a copy of Verses which I have titled 'A Farewell & Defiance to Love' & fatherd on Sir John Harrington[134] but I dont suppose they will get inserted

Wed. 3 Aug.   A person of the name of Clay came to see me the 'Editor of the Scientific Receptacle'[135] he stopt with me all the rest [of the] day he talked much of poetry & Poets but the latter were such names that nobody knew but himself the correspondents of Deweys Mathematical Companions &c &c – he told me an odd circumstance of the farmer in the fen growing nothing but 'Teazles' for the purpose of carding a nap on cloth they are stronger he says then the wild made so perhaps by cultivation

Thur. 4 Aug.   Recieved a letter from Mrs Gilchrist in which she says that Barron Field[136] has offered to edit Octave's miscellaneous papers

Tues. 9 Aug.   Sowed my Anemonie & Bath Polyanthus seed – lent Miss Fanny Knowlton Bloomfields Hazlewood Hall[137] & Remains & Aytons Essays – Got a look at Gillead [?] of Spaldings 'Alworth Abbey'[138] & I never saw such a heap of unnatural absurdities & ridiculous attempts at wit & Satire strung together in my reading existance

Wed. 10 Aug.   A Newspaper lye of the first order – 'Mr Gale of Holt in the parish of Bradford Wilts has at present a Pear of the jargonel kind in his possession which was taken by himself from the tree in 1776, 49 years ago & is now as sound as at the first moment it was gathered. It is hung up by the stalk & no means whatever has been adopted to preserve it' – it must have been a wooden one

Sat. 13 Aug.   Went to Milton wrote a Letter to Miss Kent – & corrected & sent the Proof back to Taylor – saw the transactions of the Horticultural society

Sun. 14 Aug.   Returned from Milton brought home some flower seeds & roots – saw two very large catterpillars which a man found among the Potatoes in his garden one was about 3 inches long & the other 4 the smaller one was green with triangular marks of black, light blue, & yellow,

[81]

the other was yellow with triangular marks of the same
colors as the other save that w[h]ere the other was yellow
this was white
Sat. 20 Aug.   Wrote a letter to Henderson & sent one with
it to get frankd for A A Watts Esq[139] Editor of the
'Literary Souvenir' with a Ballad 'First Loves
Reccolections' for insertion in that Work
Sun. 21 Aug.   Recievd a letter from Mr Emmerson which
tells me that Lord Radstock dyed yesterday he was the best
friend I have met with – tho he possessed too much of that
simple heartedness to be a fashionable friend or hypocrite
yet it often led him to take hypocrites for honest friends &
to take an honest man for an hypocrite –
Tues. 23 Aug.   Found a beautiful Deaths head Moth
catterpillar in Billings potatoes it is about 4½ inces long of
most beautiful rainbow colors
Fri. 26 Aug.   Recievd a letter from the Editor of a new
Annual Almanack of the Muses or Souvenir or Forget me
not or some such things intended to be published by
Messrs Baynes & Son of Paternoster Row requesting me to
send a contribution
Sat. 27 Aug.   James Billings shot a Cuckoo to day on one
of his Plumb trees – it was very like the sparrow hawk in
color but it had a strait bill & very thin short yellow legs
neither of which seemed able to turn assailants in its own
defence for it had only its wing broke & lived a long while
it peckd at the hand that was held to it but it coud not
peck so hard as a blackbird – the inside of its mouth was of
a fine red which led us to think it was a Cuckoo
Sun. 28 Aug.   Yesterday I found another of those deaths
head Moth catterpillars in Billings Potatoes
Mon. 29 Aug.   Went to Milton turned out a very wet day
took the two large catterpillars which I had found in
Billings potatoes & found they are the Deaths Head Moth
Tues. 30 Aug.   The account of Lord Radstocks death was
thus mentioned in 'Bells Weekly Messenger' of August 29th
– 'On the 17th Instant Admiral Lord Radstock was seized
at his house in Portland Place with a sudden attack of
apoplexy. The strength of his constitution struggled with
that of the malady till the 20th when the hopes which had

been entertained of his recovery vanished & his Lordship expired – Admiral Lord Radstock G.C.B. aged 72 was the second son of John third Earl of Walgrave by the Lady Elizabeth Leveson Gower sister of the Marquis of Stafford'

Fri. 2 Sept. 1825   Recieved a letter from Mrs Emmerson

Sun. 4 Sept.   Wrote a letter to Mrs Emmerson & one to Mrs Gilchrist & one also to Baynes & Son Publishers in Paternoster row respecting some contribution solicited for a new Poetical Almanack

Wed. 7 Sept.   Recievd a letter from Hessey telling me that Taylor has been very ill also one from Messrs Baynes & Son & one from Allaric A. Watts of Manchester—Recieved in October a letter from J. Power[140] of the Strand requesting permission to publish Broomsgrove with music for which he gave me 2 Sovereigns

Thur. 8 Sept.   Met old Dacon the Jew of Cliff at Billings who has the odd notion to believe himself the saviour of the world & in spite of all this is a very sensible & remarkable man – about 5′ 10 Inches high with a pleasing countenance his hair & beard is never cut or shaved

Sun. 11 Sept.   Went to meet Mr & Mrs Emmerson at the New Inn at Deeping & spent 3 days with them

Sun. 6 Feb. 1828   Read in the Examiner the Bankrupt of W. Baynes & Son so there goes £5 which I was to have had for writing in the Amulet

Mon. 7 Feb.   Greatly distressed today & uncommonly ill O what a blessing is health we know not how to prize it till we loose it Dr. Darling restored me to health but my foolish follys has compelled her to leave me again & I fear for ever

Wed. 9 Feb.   Went to Stamford today with Patty in great distress to Dr Cooper I have set it down here to see if I shall live till 1829 to see it again I fear not but so be it I am not my own maker

The Appendices

The nine appendices are:

1 Names from whom I have recieved Letters & to whom I have written [78 names]

2 Quotations from Chatterton [in pencil and very indistinct]

3 Quotations from Aaron Hill (1685–1750) [indistinct]

4 Instructions for the dedications for 'next editions' of books and for 'Remains'

5 Memorandum about money in the 'Funds' (given on p. 86)

6 Quotations from Aaron Hill's 'Poem of Love' [very indistinct]

7 Twenty-four lines – not consecutive – from *The Song of Solomon* [indistinct]

8 Short quotations – not exact – from Byron 'Coincedences &c', 'Morad Beyes Letter to Sir Sidney Smith Wilsons Egypt Abridgd Ed 1813', 'Falconers Shipwreck' (1762), 'Waller's Poem 1712', 'Peter Pindars Lousiad P. 28' [John Wolcot, 1738–1819], 'A. A. Watts in The Souvenir for 1825', 'Chatterton Ella', 'Crabbs Works'

9 'The Will o Whisp or Jack a lanthorn' (given on p. 88)

Appendix 5

There is £400 in the Funds[1] or at least was before it was put in said to be in the joint names of Taylor & Hessey I know nothing more

I have had no settlement with Taylor & Hessey yet for neither of the volumes[2] & have gone on in a very foolish manner I am sorry now tho its not too late – one of the best counselors tells me to 'put no confidence in Man' & I believe Experience is reminding me that brotherly faith is of less worth then nothing but Experience sells her advice very dear & makes every body pay for it. I understand that 7000 of the Poems on Rural Life & Scenery & the Village Minstrel was struck off up to the 4 Editions of the one & 2nd Edition of the other 5000 of the first & 2000 of the Second I was to have half the profits but I wish I had sold them out & out as others do & then I shoud have had the principal out at use & the interest to live on & now I get nothing as it were

Edward Drury has most of my M.S.S. & Taylor & Hessey has copies & originals of them all I have got few or none myself this hurts me very often no doubt they will do the right thing & yet there is many doubts they may not

I will have the Shepherds Calendar out directly – I will set down before I forget it a Memorandum to say that I desire Mrs Emmerson will do just as she pleases with any M.S.S. of mine which she may have in her possession to publish them or not as she chuses but I desire that any living names mentiond in my letters may be filld up by + + + & all objectionable passages ommitted a wish which I hope will be invariably complied with by all I also intend to make Mr Emmerson one of the Executors in my new will

I wish to lye on the North side the Churchyard i.e. just

about the middle of the ground were the Morning & Evening Sun can linger the longest on my Grave I wish to have a rough unhewn stone something in the form of a mile Stone so that the playing boys may not break it in their heedless pastimes with nothing more on it then this Inscription

HERE
Rest the
HOPES
and Ashes
of
JOHN CLARE

October
8th
1824
'Vanity of vanitys
all is Vanity'

I desire that no date be inserted thereon as I wish it to live or dye with my poems & other writings which if they have merit with posterity it will & if they have not it is not worth preserving

Memorandums Continued

I once signed an agreement made out to Drury a long while back but I was repentant afterwards of it & it was burnt I have made nor signed none since & never will Drury was to allow me a quarters profit bravo I was drunk at the time & therefore heeded not the bargain till I heard about it from my lost friend Octavius Gilchrist[3] the agreement of Drury was said to be burnt & I know nothing further But this I know that there is no other agreement in existance beyond what I have wished in my last will of Sep 1824

"o where are they stern ruin say
"then dost but eccho "were are they""
                    A. A. Watts in the Souvineir for 1825

"Jannius appears the shadow of a shade
            Byrons Vison of Judgement
"How in view what bee ye the ye asked
who shade "
                    Chillerlows Ella

"Nay creatures borrowd & again conving
"From book to book the Shadoes of a shade
                    Crabbs Works

                    No 9
The Wills whisp or Jack a lanthorn
I have often seen them or foxes on that
some philosophy may call them but I never
out used so remathkeble an instance of the
little philosophic reasons which I did —
belief phelosophic reasons which I did —
about them I now believe them spirits but
I will leave the facts to speak for themselves
— There had been a great uproar in the
town about the appearance of the ghost
of an old woman who had been nearly
drownd in a well — it was said to appear
at the bottom of neighbour Billings close
in a large stile ending sheed drift & the
noise excited the curiosity of myself
& my neighbours to go out seven at night
together to see if the ghost would be kind
enough to appear to us & mend our broken
faith in its existance but nothing came
on our return we saw a light in the north
east over eastwell green & I thought at

Appendix 9
The Will o Whisp or Jack a lanthorn

I have often seen these vapours or whatever philosophy may
call them but I never witnessed so remarkable an instance of
them as I did last night which has robd me of the little
philosophic reasoning which I had about them I now believe
them spirits but I will leave the facts to speak for themselves
– there had been a great upstir in the town[1] about the appearance of the ghost of an old woman who had been recently
drownd in a well it was said to appear at the bottom of
neighbour Billings close[2] in a large white winding sheet dress
and the noise excited the curosity of myself & my neighbour
to go out several nights together to see if the ghost would be
kind enough to appear to us & mend our broken faith in its
existance but nothing came on our return we saw a light in
the north east over eastwell green & I thought at first it was
a bright meoter[3] it presently became larger & seemd like a
light in a window it then moved & danced up & down &
then glided onward as if a man was riding on horsback at
full speed with a lanthorn light soon after this we discoverd
another rising in the south east on 'deadmoor' they was about
a furlong asunder at first & as if the other saw it it danced
away as if to join it which it soon did & after dancing together
a sort of reel as it were it chased away to its former station
& the other followd it like things at play & after suddenly
overtaking it they mingled into one in a moment or else one
disseapered & sunk in the ground we stood wondering &
gazing for a while at the odd phenomenon & then left the
willowisp dancing by itself to hunt for a fresh companion as
it chose – the night was dusky but not pitch dark & what

was rather odd for their appearance the wind blew very briskly it was full west – now these things are generally believd to be vapours rising from the foul air from bogs & wet places were they are generaly seen & being as is said lighter then the common air they float about at will – Now this is all very well for Mrs Philosophy who is very knowing but how is it if it is a vapour lighter than the air that it coud face the wind which was blowing high & always floated sideways from north to south & back – the wind afected it nothing but I leave all as I find it I have explaind the fact as well as I can – I heard the old alewife at the Exeters arms behind the church (Mrs Nottingham) often say that she has seen from one of her chamber windows as many as fifteen together dancing in & out in a company as if dancing reels & dances on eastwell moor there is a great many there – I have seen several there myself one night when returning home from Ashton on a courting excursion I saw one as if meeting me I felt very terrified & on getting to a stile I determined to wait & see if it was a person with a lanthorn or a will o whisp it came on steadily as if on the pathway & when it got near me within a poles reach perhaps as I thought it made a sudden stop as if to listen me I then believed it was someone but it blazd out like a whisp of straw & made a crackling noise like straw burning which soon convincd me of its visit the luminous haloo that spread from it was of a mysterious terrific hue & the enlargd size & whiteness of my own hands frit me the rushes appeard to have grown up as large & tall as walebone whips & the bushes seemd to be climbing the sky every thing was extorted[4] out of its own figure & magnified the darkness all round seemd to form a circular black wall & I fancied that if I took a step forward I shoud fall into a bottomless gulph which seemd yawing[5] all round me so I held fast by the stilepost till it darted away when I took to my heels & got home as fast as [I] coud so much for will o whisps.

The Essays

TASTE

Taste finds pleasure where the vulgar cannot even find amusement the man of taste feels excessive rapture in contemplating the rich scenery of an autumn Landscape which the rude man passes unnoticed – the rich colors of the forrest trees the wild hurry of the autumn clouds never harmonize his feelings into raptures – he never turns a look to the sky save in the dread of a coming shower – he never gazes on the painted wilderness of woods & hedges unless business leads his occupation thither & then his eyes is dead & sees no praise & he tramples thoughtlessly over the wooden brig that leads him on his path & never so much as glances on the stream that seems smoothening the little pebbles beneath him with its chafing gurgles he never heeds it or hears it but plods his way to the end of his intention with a mechanic impulse of uninterrupted selfishness that occupys all his little mind – to the man of discernment there is happiness in contemplating the distant shapes of leaves of the various kinds of trees plants & herbs there is happiness in examining minutely into the wild flowers as we wander amongst them to distinguish their characters & find out to what orders they belong in the artificial and natural systems of botany there is happiness in lolling over the old shivered trunks & fragments of a ruined tree destroyed some years since by lightening & mossing & wasting away into everlasting decay – to wander among the hills & hollows of heaths which have been old stone quarrys roman excavations & other matter of fact fancys that the mind delights to indulge in in rambles – this is happiness – to lean on the rail of wooden brigs & mark the crinkles of the stream below & the little dancing beetles thwarting & glancing their glossy coats to the summer sun – to bend over the old woods mossy rails & list the call of the heavy bumble bee playing with the coy flowers till he has lost his way – & anon finds it by accident & sings out of the wood to the sunshine that leads him to his mossy nest[1] lapt up in the long grass of some quiet nook – such is happiness & to wander a pathless way thro the intricays of woods for a long while & at last burst unlooked for into the light of an extensive prospect at its side & there lye & muse on the landscape to rest ones wanderings – this is real happiness – to stand & muse upon the bank of a meadow pool fringed with reed & bulrushes & silver clear in the middle of which the sun is reflected in spangles & there to listen is a luxury of happiness & felt even by the poor shepherd boy

ON PRIDE

Pride is a failing always & an ornament never when it is the attendant of riches it betokens ignorance when of poverty hypocrisy & in the man of power tyranny for with the rich it becomes a worthless assumption with the poor a needless pretention & with the man in power an overbearing scorn & obstinat arrogance for proud people look down upon the habits of the poor & 'think these shames' but the wise know them to be the trials of adversity & give them honourable notice not the cold moving nod but the freedom of equallity that alows without noticing it the rights & libertys of man to man – It is the attendant of wealth often & of insolence always where it insults worth in the garb of poverty & worships villainy in the robes of power Yet altho it is often the deciple of wealth it is never the attendant of wisdom for if wealth & pride constituted wisdom thousands might be ashamed of being poor but as wisdom does not go by heirship with rich wills & large estates many more have juster cause to be ashamed of being rich but pride gives such consciet & consciet imagines itself wisdom – thus it appears as pride is often the companion of weak & rich people it is not to be inferred from that that it is worth immitating or coveting by those who are poor for we always see the most foolish proud & that is the very reason why wise men consider pride a folly & learn to despise it – for on the other hand if a wise man happens to be a rich man we see him affable in his bearing humble in his pretentions & condescending to all ranks & conditions of men the king & the beggar have no further distinction of rank in his mind than that of man to man & he treats the one with the respect he merits & the other with the kindness he deserves & thus he gains a lasting & universal esteem where esteem only is worth having & not for the pride & authority he can show but for showing that he is too wise to show that authority not for learning & knowledge in books & language but the modest feeling of believing himself ignorant of true learning for the more a man learns the less reason he finds to be proud & thus a man learns to feel that he still knows nothing This makes him humble ready to learn not looking for homage but instruction not for being a gentleman with great riches titles & great heraldic distinctions of nobility but for showing by his affability modesty & simplicity that he would have been & is a gentleman without them thus it is that the presense of pure nobility always creates less fear then esteem & more confidence of respect then dread to offend – It is not the laced coat that makes wisdom the good man or the star & garter that makes the gentleman but it is the cultivation of the mind that makes both – & such men have no pride further then the nobleness to treat pride & its pretentions with contempt these set the great example to others to despise pride in their inferiors & pity it in their superiors for pride cannot make itself superior in anything as it levels all distinctions to the lowest grades & makes a beggar of nobility by showing that it is poor in the commonest inheritance & the proudest nobility of man – wisdom & commonsense – for commonsense is the wisdom of necessity & he who hath either despises pride which hath neither this is the reason why fools only are proud & wise men nearer a wisdom which every one who feels himself worthy the name of man ought [to] feel the nessesity to learn & an example which everyone who wishes to be respectable

& esteemed ought to practise & follow for 'it is a great pride' saith the divine to think we have no pride as that is to think we are as good indeed as we esteem ourselves 'But there is no man in the world but esteems himself better than he truly is'. Therefore it is our constant duty to strive to be as wise & as good as we can & he who humbles his own pride makes the best resolve to be wise

ON INDUSTRY

Industry being the goddess of thrift many restless people would fain believe themselves industrious when they are not for industrious people should be contented people pursuing those avocations only by which they are sure of a livelihood but the restless & discontented person pursues many vision-ary avocations by which at best he only hopes to thrive not feeling that it is best to be sure of living first & speculating afterwards & thus failing in their purposes they murmur at fortune & consider themselves unfortunates in the end but these people place the saddle on the wrong horse seldom or ever having anything to blame but themselves – an old man who was very anxious after riches & yet always poor tho not idle altho he possesd a very odd notion & a propensity that haunted him thro life of hoping to find lost or hidden treasures & wether he was at his toils or on a journey he was always plodding along with his head downwards watching the ground in hopes of finding an old earthern pot peeping above the soil under his plough full of old coin or a bag upon his path crammed with guineas people who always saw him in this musing mood thought him a very studious man & used to fancy him a philosopher but saving the hopes after lost money he had never another occupation for thinking in his heart & as he never found any his head may have been said to be entirely empty both of thought & philosophy One morning as he was journeying home thro a large tract of uncultivated wilderness called the Black Forrest no doubt from its gloomy grandeur & uncivilised extent still nourishing his long cherished hopes after lost money he reccolected

hearing people often talk about money being buried there
& in one spot in particular tho he knew not where to find it
he had been told that some forresters had accidently discovered a well in this forrest & in the well a large Iron pot which
they had nearly hauled up to the top when one of them
happening to swear at the weight of it it instantly became too
heavy for their strength & fell down to the bottom & was
never recovered afterwards Yet he had heard of rich knights
living there centurys back in large castles that were now level
with the ground & he thought these the most likely spots he
could hit upon to search for it & the hopes of finding it grew
so strong & so likely that he determined to lose a day &
proceed to one of these ridges where Castles or Halls had
most undoubtedly stood & having a new spade which he had
been on purpose to purchase & he thought this a lucky
incident & a better token or prospect of success so he went
to an old ridgy spot on which the brushwood could hardly
flourish from the many stones & rubbish that lay beneath
them so that the identity of something having been there was
thus confirmed & further by its being called Robin Hoods
Castle so he dug away & laboured along while sometimes
finding glass beeds sometimes bits of curious pottery & fragments of ornamented stones but he could not find the old
pot of money he sought for tho he picked up two or three
bits of old coin which his anxiety almost hear[d] the 'old pot'
knock against the corner of his spade until by rubbing them
on the edge of his knife he found them neither gold nor silver
& tho this discovery dissapointed his anxietys a moment it
wetted his hopes with a keener relish after lost treasures so
he still dug on amongst the stones & rubbish untill hunger
made him weary & on looking up for the sun he found it
(to his suprise) far in the west hastening to bed & he very
reluctantly [ ]² from his search wishing to be home before
nightfall but he determined to come agen the next morning
as he fancied by finding the few base coins that he had
verrified the old proverb 'Where theres dirt theres money'
& fancying that the old kettle of gold was not far from the
spot he determined to turn back & just try an half hour
longer for he thought it a pity after his days labour to let
another body run away with the prize when to his supprise

& astonishment he found an old man busily looking among
the rubbish which he had thrown up & suspecting this was
none other than the Old man of the Forrest he almost feared
to approach him yet knowing that he had never used any bad
words in his labours like the forresters at the well & flushed
with the hopes [of] getting his assistance to hunt the ruins he
ventured to offer a question as to the purpose of his search
& assured him there was nothing there as he had just thrown
it up & searched it all over but the old man of the forrest
(for sure enough it was none other) looked up & with a smile
searched on without deigning to reply appearing too busy
for discourse & at length to the old money hunters supprise
who thought a part of the money pot he turned up a hugh
piece of somthing either of Iron or Steel in the shape of a
large wedge this said the old man of the desert is the only
treasure in this place worth looking for or finding & as thou
hast a desire to be rich I will give it thee but take care to
heed this advice Clean it carefully from rust & then devise
the best way to keep it clean for by keeping it clean thou
shalt get more riches then are burried in this whole forrest
& the old mans heart leapt up with astonishment & gladness
as he recieved the present for he knew the tales of his fore-
fathers that to win the favours of the old man of the forrest
was a certain prelude to riches & happiness & he was for
thanking him a thousand times when the old man stopt him
by observing that if he did not find out the best way to keep
it clean properly after he had once cleaned it it was not worth
thank ye but if it once got rusty it had been better for him
never to accept it as it would be a token of his poverty as
long as he lived so the old man determined on keeping it
clean & thanking the old man of the forrest & bidding him
farwell he hastened home with his singular prize glad at least
yet wishing it had been the pot of money instead of it for he
could not help wishing & when he displayed it to his astonished wife she could not tell what to make of it but when he
had written down the advice of the old man that he might
never forget it they being both simple bodies put their wisdom together & exerting every inch they possesed to the
utmost pitch they determined at last to clean it directly –
they were very frugal withal & they both had a great desire

to obtain money & yet withal their frugality they never could
find the way to get it & tho the desire never made them
unhappy it always made them frugal & striving to be saving
thus both were alike anxious to clean the piece of 'old rusty
iron' & began in right earnest to rub off the thick crust of
rust & when they had got it clean thus far it was as black as
ever but riches haunting both their imaginations was a re-
sistless spur to their labours & after a tedious series of rub-
bings & scourings the piece of old rusty iron was as bright
& clean as the fire iron which hung in the corner & they
were both all raptures & expectations tho their wits were
now puzzled to the utmost to find out the best way to keep
it clean & after many devisings they concluded that the best
preservative to keep it from damps & consequently from rust
was to hang it up among the fire irons in the corner & there
it hung the daily hope of the old lady & the hourly expectation of the old man but still no money came for the simple
old man still expecting that the money was to be found
looked for his luck on the ground with unremitting assuidity
whenever he happened to be employed at his labour or journeying at his leisure & tho the piece of old iron still hung up
among the fire irons undergoing with them weekly scourings
so that a spot of rust was never found upon it after it entered
the cottage yet to their supprise they never could find themselves sixpence the better for it all their lives & the old man
lived & dyed as poor as he was when he dug for lost treasures
in the ruins of Robin Hoods castle & he left an only son
behind him as poor as himself with the only legacy of the
old iron & the advice to employ the best methods to keep it
clean & tho the people laughed at the weakness & superstitions of the simple old man in indulging & believing in such
fancys yet the son thought differently & tho he shared a
portion of his fathers superstitions he had a more enterprizing
spirit & when they called him the young philosopher in
derisision of his fathers infirmitys Time proved that they gave
him not a wrong name tho it was not a right one for his
father – the right way to keep it clean always attracted his
notice & made him fancy that the best way as yet had not
been employed nor could he think of cleaning it every week
to hang up in the corner as his parents had done for his

restless spirit could find no time waste being ever anxiously employed after more profitable labours & so he argued with himself that the old man of the forrest would not have any reason to be offended with him if in trying to correct his fathers errors he did not find out the best way but declaring that as he had no time on his hands to waste over cleaning it as they had done he resolved to make it clean itself by beating it into the share of his Plough & when he had done so his reverence for & unshaken faith in the Legends of the old man of the forrest gave him such anxiety to please the old man & such fear to offend him that he was never comfortable but when at labour with his plough determining to keep it free from rust at all events & to leave the rest to the old man of the forrest so by this means his little farm soon became the theme of astonishment & praise in the eyes of his friends & the envy of his neighbours for by constant tillage every weed was destroyed & the crops yielded a double increase people who had land near his farm to let were ever anxious for him to take it & by this means he got a good farm & riches began to increase with his means untill at last he was justly considerd the largest & most oppulent farmer in the county & from his success people who had laughed at the simple superstitions of his father grew more superstitious themselves & everybody was for looking on their way not only for money but for old iron as it grew into a saying that it was lucky to find it & unlucky to pass bye it as every bit thus passed might be some of the identical ore belonging to the old man of the Forrest so the villagers gathered up all the old iron they found yet none ever after gathered the right as they never got rich by their findings For industry alone is the mother of. wealth & frugality the mother of comfort & these two are the parents of honesty & happiness for so the lucky son found it when he discovered the best way to keep clean the gift of the Old man of the forrest

ON HAPPINESS

Some people are weak enough to guess & fancy that happiness is nothing less then the possesions of wealth & few give themselves the trouble to prove & be sure that happiness is nothing more then the enjoyment of contentment for it has been often said that our wants increase with our means but it is a truer fact that our wants increase faster then our means & instead of leading to prosperity often leaves us in embarrasments – A young fisherman who lived near the sea was very industrious & very thriving in his industry but he thirsted after more wealth the possesion of which was his happiness he lived in [a] comfortable cottage but he thought happiness dwelt in a pallace so when he did ever so well he wished to do better he was ever merry as a fisherman but he thought he should be more happy as a gentleman when he was poor he thought that a new suit of cloaths would even make him one & he soon procured these from the success of his calling he found he must purchase his cottage before he was independant this he was enabled to do very quickly by having the luck in a wreck harvest to find a sum of money that made the purchase he then all of a sudden discovered that he wanted a new boat before he was quite set up & this he was not long in acquiring for on sailing away in his boat one fine morning to pursue his usual avocations full of his fortunate fancys & scraps of old songs he accidenteoraly saw an old man in a fine new boat approaching rapidly towards him The young man was going speedily with wind & tide but the old man was going more speedily against both & the young fisherman was astonished & he thought to himself this is just the boat I want to be next to a gentleman – Is it said the old man whose voice whistled in his ear as sharp as the wind in the canvas of a top gallant & the young fisherman was more astonished still for his wishes had never rose so loud as a whisper yet the old man heard them & if you should like my boat continued he you shall have it in exchange for yours & if you mind you may then very soon be a gentleman tho for my part I would rather have your lot now then that of a gentlemans hereafter for remember said the old man the gods give mortals the liberty to amass riches but leave the use of them entirely to their own discretion & what is one mans food is another mans poison as wishes generally get the start of & encroach upon pleasures – I change said the young man loosing his fear in his satisfaction & cutting the advice

of the old man in the middle without considering the end
& the old man laughed aloud as he leapt into the young mans
boat but as the young man got into his with as evident
satisfaction the old man shook his head when he bade him
good speed – & they instantly parted the old man speeding
a horse gallop with wind & tide & the young man at double
speed against both – he was highly delighted but reccolecting
all of a sudden that he was going the very contrary way to
that which he intended to proceed he instantly seized the
rudder to manage the boat the right way when to his utter
astonishment the boat shot plump down & down & down
into the very bottom of the sea as fast as a race horse could
gallop from the top of mount atlas into the vallies beneath it
& even faster went the young man & his boat down & down
untill he rested on the very bottom of the immense ocean
& he was astonished even above fear when he saw the waters
for miles above about him & yet he breathed as free from
choaking as he did before he started from the greensward
bench beside the door of his own cottage How it could be
he could not tell but so it was & as his eyes began to clear
of their suprise he began to look about him to see the strange
country he was in & every thing was new & nothing &
nothing like what he had seen before There were large forrests
as high as those upon earth but of very different colours &
when he came to examine them he fancied they were of pearl
& coral & rubies & emeralds there were also monsters of
extraordinary size & shape he recollected descriptions of
heaven in the bible & what he had never expected to encounter & thought for a surety that it could be nowhere else
but at the bottom of the sea men & women approached him
not very handsome these where to be sure for they had green
hair & red eyes & teeth of rather awkward dimentions yet
they seemed young & well shaped he accosted them but they
could not understand his language or he theirs & they were
amusing themselves in a variety of way[s] but a young maiden
astonished him the most was entertaining her leisure with
forming grottos of dollars & nobles & guineas & all manner
of coins in gold & silver & he was happy enough after much
perplexity to make her understand that he admired her ma-
terials even more then her skill whereupon she instantly fell

[100]

to filling his boat with the treasure & soon had a train of assistance from her companions so as to fill the boat with the gold & silver which seemed as bright as if minted but yesterday & lying all this time leaning on his rudder he in the absolute triumph of his heart clapped his hands together & exclaimed now Im a gentleman & the boat sprang upward (as his hands left the rudder) as light as an egg shell so that he was at top before he had finished the sentence & at the mooring beside his own door before he could have repeated it & leaping ashore he was speedily engaged at unlading his treasures his wife grew fearful at the sight of much treasure & more terrified when he related the story as to how he obtained it so he resolved on keeping the extent of his treasure a mystery to her perplexity for all she could think of was that the better way was to be out of it & return [it] from where it came to the bottom of the sea & perhaps she was not far from right for if ever we recieve a great favour from fortune we seldom make use of it as if it was the last we should meet with but on the contrary only consider it as the first we have recieved but he called the advice of his wife nothing but down right foolishness & felt to inform himself of the extent of his treasure he counted & counted & then made all safe to count again & it was at last all to no purpose for it seemed without number & without end so he secured it uncounted & before he went to bed a thought struck him to secure the boat also by taking away the rudder into his cottage (having by this time fully discovered that this was the principle charm to his lucky adventure in the strange boat) & thinking that the old man of the sea might call again in the night for his boat & exchange it he resolved upon this to prevent him – The young fisherman thinking the old man had good reasons for changing his mind he resolved he should keep it but the old Man never seemed to regret anything about the bargain for he left the boat unmolested with its present owner who was now a gentleman & he was determined to act up to the title for he laid up his boat for a season & gave up fishing as he hoped for ever & looked out for amusements suitable to his station & his altered condition soon got into full cry like a fox chase & the county round was running over with guesses & surmises as to how he got his money which was wasted in hasty speculations & scattered after foolish bargains like chaff in the wind as he knew there was plenty where that came from he first bought a horse & then he coveted a gig & then he resolved on a coach & with those expansive matters crowds of expenses followed as nessesary attendants & many cunning bargain hunters followed in the train & a host of friends added to the number to waste his fortune & share in the spoils & as his extravagant notions kept increasing with his extravagant expenditure he at length determined on building a ship & becoming merchant & these large thoughts just grew up into his mind as the last of his treasure became exausted which gave him no manner of trouble knowing there was more where that came from so he went out with his rudder & off with his boat to sea where he was not long deliberating before he laid hold of it & down he went to the bottom swifter then a shooting star from the sky but unluckily for him he found this was not the spot on which he at first alighted nor could he find it if he had tried as there was nothing on the sea to mark & if he had considered this in time he would not have depended too much on chances as they will decieve us for success is not constant nor good luck everlasting but he thought nothing about the matter so he went on adventures at a venture & was dissapointed for the spot he was now in was quite different to the spot he was in before – the monsters were more numerous but much less & the groves of corral no larger then bushes here was no sea nymphs or any grottos of Dollars & guineas that betokened any success to his voyage he who is too eager in pursuit catches no game at length a numerous troop of creatures shaped like childern tho of strange complexions made their appearance rolling large bundles of somthing lapped in canvas before them in which the gingling of money assailed his ears & on his making his wishes known by signs they quickly filled his boat with the booty which by the noise made as they fell in it he was sure was money so when his boat would hold no more he left the rudder & spun up to the top like an air bubble from the mouth of a whale & himself & his boat was as usual at its moorings & he in his cottage with his treasure as quick as a wish for the better & as eager as a hope of success to unload & unlap his treasures for he had a large

ship to build & the mansion worthy of a merchant to erect
& a many more great things all of which he might readily
have done before instead of doing what he did but these he
resolved to set about tomorrow but the resolves of to day
are often the bankrupts of tomorrow & the lucky tomorrow
often expires before the end of today He opened his treasures
& they were all nothing but halfpence this as a first finding
would have been considered a good finding but now it was
a nothing for our wants increase with our means so fast that
our means tho great will not in the end support them so he
felt exceeding sorrowfull for his hopes of a ship was a wreck
& his merchants house was in ruins for his present treasure
tho much would not above pay his nessesary expences & he
felt sorry now that he had spent the other so heedlessly &
resolved to spend this more frugally dismissing the greater
portion of his friends whom he never ought to have considered further then his acquaintance & he now found when
he had not enough that we ought to take care & contrive to
keep what we have gotten before we look to get more This
he should have thought of when he had plenty but the fisherman like the rest of us paid dear for experience who like
the old proverb resolved to lock up the stable when the horse
was stolen & feeling assured that he could get halfpence
enough to last if nothing else to turn merchant so he went
out with his boat & instead of turning to his old occupation
of fishing he determined to go out daily a money catching
hoping to get his old hawl of guineas & crowns & felt sure
of his copper so he sailed out as on his first voyage much
further to sea & to be sure that he was far enough he went
further still so taking hold of the rudder he was down in a
moment were he found as on his first voyage corral forrests
of much larger dimensions & monsters of greater bulk so
great that they were like mountains & he almost dreaded that
they would overwhelm boat & all yet he felt it his duty &
more his nessesity to wait for the greenhaired ladys & a
company of grotesque resemblances to the human form was
seen advancing in the distance amusing themselves with carrying large box or tub shaped vessels to build grottos or
cottages for they were of immense statue[3] & as he heard
money chink in his mind as they advanced he worked up the

[103]

best of his wits to win a boat load of their prizes nor was he long in making his wishes understood for they immediately on approaching his boat fell to filling it with their loads untill he had scarcely room enough left to stand in & he felt exceedingly happy & burst out now for the ship & the pallace for as they rolled them over the side of the boat he heard the guineas ring as loud as a fire bell & he gave the sea Ladies time to upheap the boat before he layed hold of the rudder when he was up & ashore with his load in the hairspace of a moment when he wrote out the orders for building the ship & the merchant house & sent them off before he had even time to open the treasures but when he did try this he was astonished to find that which rung louder in his mind then ever did a guinea before was only a liquid & he was all down to his shoes in dissapointment tho by tasting he found it was the very best of Brandy & the custom house officers were soon at his heels who made him unlade it & finding it was a smuggled cargo they instantly took him into custody while he vainly protested his innocence that he was no smuggler The charmed boat became forfieted & he a prisoner to the laws of the country & wether the custom house officers ever discovered the secret powers of the charmed boat nobody ever knew but it was speedily discovered that the chief officer of the gang grew rich & tho he did not procure coaches or build ships or pallaces he suddenly retired from his profession altogether & what became of the boat is not known for the poor Fisherman never recovered it – having been retained in prison for debt & set at liberty just soon enough to find that he had not a farthing left in the world as his House & land followed the fate of his boat & was sold to satisfy the rapacious demands of his friends in prosperity and his creditors in adversity & the only thing he had left him was his hope to get a livelihood again by following his old trade of a fisherman & experience tho dear bought had taught him one thing to his comfort that content was happiness & not money or pallaces & he who reads the fate of the Fisherman may get his experience for nothing & turn the profit to account for mind it is as true a tale as ever was written let me repeat that Content is happiness & again caution the reader that the tale however strange is no fiction & if he reads rightly he will discover that however good it may seem to begin well it will turn out a much better good to end well

There is truth even in its fictions for they are typical mysteries of a restless mind & what is more fictitious then its pursuits & more wild then its ambitions

ON AFFECTATION

Motto
It is the witness still of excellency
To put a strange face on his own perfection

There are many follys & all contemptible ones but the folly of affectation is the most ridiculous of any – I was once invited to join a tea party at the house of a friends acquaintance where the good people possesed a pretty daughter in the shape of a pert forward girl who said & did every thing with the greatest self possesion imaginable she was considered pretty by her acquaintance & very handsome by her parents & herself & further she was quite a genius & affected in everything – I observed she laughed at everything or indeed when there appeared nothing to laugh at or in any way tickling to the rest of the company for she seemed determined to keep laughing which she did in a very mechanical & unfeeling manner as if something more then happiness was the cause for she rather grinned the[n] laughed & when any thing occured that caused the rest to laugh heartily she only forced the cold smile & grin as usual but I discovered that these smiles or lip drillings discovered a beautiful set of teeth & I soon found that the grinning smiles was for the purpose of showing them & not from the accident of being suddenly pleased or delighted with any thing that occured in her hearing that like the Sempstress in the Idler 'The baggage had got a trick of smiling' & a many other tricks to which the Sempstress had no pretention The mother called her a genius of the first order in everything & the father affirmed that she was so & they began to extol her pretentions even before we were seated tho I was a perfect stranger she was a sort of 'actor of

all work' & excelled in everything – she painted exquisitly
wrote charmingly played on the Piano beautifully sung de-
lightfully & spouted Shakespear admirably superior even to
Kean so said the lady her mother & the young lady instead
of shrinking from such praises before a stranger into the
modesty of virgin timidity like as the beauty of the evening
primrose from the gaze of the morning sun she became like
the gaudy sunflower enarmoured of the lustre of such glaring
praises & all prepared for the profession of display in the
phrase of the Showman 'ready to begin' & as if the subject
was got up on purpose for exebition She began to discourse
first on painting & ran over a catalouge of the old masters
with all the unembarassed readiness of an auctioneer & she
extolled their beautys & touched upon their different styles
with the tact & presumption of a picturedealer & I thought
to be sure she was a painter of excellence from her discoursing
so readily but when she was getting into the climax of the art
of flourishing over her own beauty in the luxurant beautys
of Rapha⁴ Turner she unexpectly turned to the Chinese painting & after to my astonishment lauding it up as equsite⁵ &
worthy of all praise she stopt the matter suddenly & her
mother like a good & attentive scene shifter knowing the first
act was concluded opening a drawer in the Bureau at her
elbow brought out two large designs for firescreens all of her
daughters workmanship as she expressed it & both looked
all expectation for admiration my friend coughed over his
shoulder as if dreading the attack of being first to admire &
I wishing to say something handsome spilt my tea all over
the one that was laid on the table for approbation as I awk-
ardly bent over it under the pretention of a closer inspection
but with the real intention of getting an oppertunity to pause
to think how to express my praise in the least ridiculous
manner – my hand forgot the cup which it held & my head
being busy with the search after complements forgot every
thing else & bending to the picture my flowery cup bent also
& down went the scalding tea over the bald heads of the
mandarins – my embarrassment was terrible & the young
ladys temper grew as terrible for she snatched up the drawing
& fled into the next room to encourage her passion against
me saying loud enough to be heard that a many boorish

people handled paintings as carless & awkard as a clown handled the wrappers of soap & candles & that a work worth twenty guineas was destroyed beyond the recovery of a farthing – while the old lady was almost in hysterics but my friend who still held the other drawing in his hand soon brought matters to rights & seeing my confusion extolled the painting most fluently the old lady was all raptures & her daughter came round from her passion with an affability to retake her chair & even to ask my opinion There was blue trees pink skyes mountains of white lead & valleys of yellow ochre & added to this incongruous mixture of internal colouring the perspective was even more unnatural then the coloring & a green wicker work sort of bridge over a river of brickdust in the distance was of larger proportions than a green house in the foreground & the bunch tailed figure of a mandarin or chinese shepherd on the farthest peak of the farthest white mountain was larger then both the bridge & the pallace put together but to get over the confusion I had unfortunately created I praised & with friendly assistance pointed out the brightness of the colours the goodness of the paper & origeonality of the design tho the very China teacups out of which we were drinking afterwards discovered to us the pattern of those celebrated fire screens whose bad perspective & incongruous harmony of colouring she had so faithfully copied as to make the copy display a worse taste then the origional – our praise encouraged the subject & we were shown Landscapes buildings flowers & cattle studies hung round the room in clusters & ornamented with fine gilt frames & peering thro exellent glasses we could not of course enter into the particulars of every production but one in particular was shown us as the chief d'ouver[6] of her daughters tallents it was a needle work St Paul preaching at Athens in a coarse garment of green worsted & stockings of red silk the harmony of colouring even surpassing the chinese Mandarins on the firescreens my friend said he knew nothing of needlework & the matter dropt rather luckily from painting altogether. We was then elevated into poetry & the young lady repeated her own production as ready & with as little hesitation as the school boy turning over his task This was on 'a favourite animal' & a sort of new version of 'poor Colly

[107]

my cow' The red spots on her 'pretty coat' & her 'curly horns' were as largely noted & as punctually attended too as they were in her portrait over the chimney – the poem of one hundred lines she declared (after she had repeated it) was written ryhmed & all to a minute within the hour for a wager with her father who thought it impossible for even genius to do & when she looked over it for corrections she found only two mistakes the lady declared all was fact & her father had bestowed on her a gold watch as the prize so like [ ]⁷ they were golden verses & taking silence for admiration & astonishment the old proceeded with the consent of the young one to show us her album several pages of which contained a compleat catalogue of the Epitaphs in the church yard which to show her readiness at her pen as well as pencil was printed in a note to be all copied in two hours precisely here too was some very curious items of autographs of literary farmers & graziers with accounts of the largest trees in England & the largest oxen ever seen in the shows at smithfield with wonders of calves with three heads & chickens with three legs & other monsters with mottos for garden benches hourglasses & samplers & such like attributes of excellence & all the time she kept quoting the poets occasionaly & the Poet (Shakespear) constantly & particularly not from her fondness for Shakespear as might be easily discoverd but for the showing off beauty in a taste for the fine Arts & womanly excellence in the appearance of a masculine mind to comprehend & appreciate the great excellances of the greatest poet among men & she let not the most trifling oppertunity slip of turning the most trifling accident to advantage by applying a quotation to illustrate it with such ready wit & graceful adaption that would even raise molehills to mountains & drowned mice to the consequence of dead lions Her father who sat sleeping most of the time in an easy chair happening to reccolect that the carpenter had not had notice that he was to come to make some repairs about the premises in the morning the young lady instantly reccolected & repeated the clowns riddle in Shakespear to show her extensive & happy powers of memory because a carpenter was mentioned in it The old lady expressed her astonishment & looked up for ours also but the old man smiled & took up his pipe for

[108]

another whiff declaring he was not supprised at all as she was capable of any thing — after this a mellancholly incident happened in the dairy as if on purpose & the servant with sorrow in her countenance came in with a poor favourite kitten that had been drowned in a milk pansion the young lady was just in the sublimity of her powers doing a scene of Keans Richard to the life & as she paused to bemoan its tragic end the old lady urged her to go on & consoled her sorrow by saying it would be an excellent oppertunity for an elegy & she instantly revived & gave us the conclusion & several other specimens she also quoted a few common shreds of latin tho my friend declared she knew not a word of the language she was a fine girl but her pertness at all knowledge of every thing & about every thing threw a disagreeable foil over her beauty for the lovely simplicity & shrinking modesty of woman is lost in the assumption to over much learning & a young girl pretending to quote latin seems as incongruous to the sex in her situation as it would be for a religious lady to be placed in the pulpit in a bishops gown or a court beauty taking presedence of office in a chancellors wig

She placed herself unbid at her piano & thumped it most charmingly singing a song of her own writing which she had paid for being set to music by a professor & she got so high in her notes & her extacy that she actualy screamed to a conclusion & then retreated to show up her specimen of Entomology for she too had got the fashionable mania to gibbet butterflyes & strangle beetles telling us the while that tho it was not generally known she had discovered that the catterpillar changed into a moth & the moth migrated into a butterfly & after this illustrious blunder she considered herself a philosopher also — my friend after we returned home expatiated largely on the folly of people showing off to such ridiculous excesses & repeated the following quotation from Montesquieu as a moral to our evenings tedious amusement 'happy is he who has vanity enough never to speak any good of himself who distrusts his hearers & avoids bringing his merits into colission with their self love'

ON HONOUR

Tis the mind that makes the body rich
& as the mind breaks through the darkest clouds
So honour peereth in the meanest habit

Honour among the superficial observers of mankind consists
in the possesion of high sounding titles & the occupation of
high apointments with the world 'nobility' is honour because
'right honourable' is its precedence so is power because the
honourable is his distinction but these are as 'sounding brass'
where there is nothing else to support them The honour of
pride is distinction & the honour of wisdom merit & the
honours of pride are pomp and ambition & their value has
nothing out at interest with time there is nothing lasting
about them they are all annuals & like that plant of Mexico
blossoms but for a few hours but the honours of merit are
mostly perennials & like the Aloe blossom once in a century
in the cold climate of reward waxing vigerous with time &
striking a deep root into the heart of emulation that is for
eternity – Shakespear & Drayton & Drake & other eternals
are the right honourables which time selected from the illustrious among the reign of Elizabeth tho she did not go to the
court calendar to find them for time is himself a kingmaker
& a creator of honours & titles

The phantoms of honour & the mock suns of greatness
must shine in their springtide or not at all They have no
summer ripeness they are found in the misty exuberance of
honours morning phantasy not in its noonday distinctions
they are the will o the wisps of splendours that magnifye
their little light from the darkness of flattery which surrounds
them for however they may shine in courts or share in the
freedom of pallaces however they may be favoured by ap-
pointments or exalted by power flattery is the only soil that
nourishes their greatness & the moment they are left to im-
partiality of opinion & time that moment like the rainbow
without the sun their brilliant colours are lost & they perish
thus these favourites of courts & pallaces who wear the livery
& not the merit of honour having nothing left to distinguish
them from the commonality of men are no longer known

& if time stumbles over their names ever after he in Satanical astonishment alters the question who were these This feeling urged Cato to declare that he had much rather posterity should enquire why no statues were raised to his memory then why they were – False honours are won by favours & favours are gained by many causes in living honours but time only alows favour to one & that is merit he has no knowledge of the person gone but the works & merits left behind him

Titles & distinctions are often inherited by the servility to superiors in power who command their flattery & even their honesty to subvert as they chuse & to whom still they are servile inferiors These may be defined as the insults of honours for where pride or power justly demands praise & from inferiors it cuts deeper then satire in the ridicule & scorn of others above the grand chorus – a person placed on the Alps would consider the people beneath him in the valleys as mere pigmys by their size & at the same time forgets that he himself is seen as a pigmy by them thus it ever is with the honours of pride where there is nothing else to reccomend them – Honours come also by heirship & often to lesser spirits gifted with fewer qualifications to recieve the dignity & no merits to consider on them but honours by merit are earned by the dignity of the possesors themselves which as the jewel in the crown constitutes its value to the latest generations This may be considered as the sun in the firmament of honour giving light to the others which are only its satellites & without which would have had no lustre of its own to distinguish it from the commonality among mankind – Honour is due to personal merit alone not to birth 'God alone is good without a name' Titles neither add to honours or take from them Blake is as great a warrior as Nelson tho one was honoured with titles & the other not & Dryden is as great as Byron tho one is plain John & the other my lord Titles are more common then honours & thus it is that there are more new patents of nobility found in a page of the court calendar every reign then there will be Shakespears & Miltons in the world from the beginning of time to that of eternity – These illustrious obscuritys those 'paper hangings' for living names with the flourishes of K.C.Bs & a hundred other important letters that swell the alphabet into magnificence

[111]

& mystified greatness however they may adorn mortality become superfluous absurditys to the eternitys Bacon G.C.B. would sound foolish & seem no honour at all & many illustrious ornaments of foreign greatness would become ridiculous associated with real greatness a Chinese nobleman of 2 feathers may sound honourable in China & a beshaw[8] of 3 tails may be very redolent of greatness in turkey but even to conceive the outoway idea of a Milton of two feathers or a Shakespear of 3 tails is rank with the stink of nonsense & becomes the personification of the ridiculous at once & custom alone reconsiles such things into the notions of honourable for could we see them in their naked oddity they would all apear as one absurdity Thus the real honours of merit are touch stones wherebye the mock honours of parade become ridiculous they are but the sweepings of honours temple & drop under the feet of time with escutcheons tombs epitaphs & other rubbish of ambitions that where[9] & thus it is that the plean simple laurel leaves wreathed around the Homers & Dantes & Shakespears of immortality have won more lasting honours then all the crowns & stars & garters of earths sovereign royaltys put together – Honour is no more to be attained from high apointments alone then it is to be degraded by mean employments a mans actions are his honours or dishonours not his names & occupations nobleness of mind debases the asumptions of meanness into contempt but littleness gives an altitude to superior beings when placed by its side as a dwarf magnifys the statue of a jiant & no greater illustration of this truth can be adduced then the noble behaviour of a greek general who after a great victory unjustly recieved the displeasure of his country for his reward who thinking to insult him voted him to the office of head scavenger to the city which in the short sighted follys of pride was most degrading to honour but he was not a man of pride or titles only these formed not the stuff he was made of & he gladly accepted it with this pride shaming & remarkable saying 'I do not wish to recieve honour from any office or apointment but I will give it dignity' & no doubt the office of city scavenger became an honourable & envied occupation instead of a degrading employment & thus are honours conferred & it is such men as Epomander[10] only that create

[112]

honour as well as confer it for the names of nobility would
be no more then the names of beggars if great men had not
chronicled such names with the assosiations of great & noble
actions & thus personified with mighty distinctions they
stamp a patent on nobility & throw a new shine on power
– that otherwise had been nothings – Insults & attempts to
degrade true honours only serve to advance it like the sun-
burst from a cloud it shines more dazzling from the disper-
sion of darkness that surrounded it Thus the actions of our
english Epomonidas[10] Blake the greatest warior of modern
times shine as brilliant in history as those heroes of antiquity
tho his name received no titles from his country & his grave
was insulted by the displeasure of a king yet his country
shares the merits of his renoun & the shame of insulting his
memory stains even the robes of majesty with meaness that
would only have been expected from a savage but flattery in
all ages & all countrys has always been found low enough in
meaness & degradations even in courts to commend the dis-
honourable actions of power as honourable & encourage the
crueltys of a tyrant as actions becoming the dignitys of majesty – it is a heart stirring & an emulating glory to discover
that the brave actions of great men always get honoured by
time while it is a degrading shame to acknowledge that the
insult offered to their merits always belong to their country
– yet thus comes the satisfaction & the victory of true honour
& nobility when the merits of the brave man triumph over
the injustice of the base one – when time finds in the one
great actions & brave deeds only recorded for the spots are
lost in the sum & nothing to record of the other but meanness
baseness & ingratitude – great men born to the honours of
time have always very contemptible enemies to anoy them
but such anomolies are natures common occurences for we
see even a contemptible flye torture the noble horse into fury
without his being able to remedy the insult from the insig-
nificance of his enemy & so are the enemys of the heroe too
trifling to notice as these paltry enemys which give their first
appearances such great annoyances cannot touch them in the
zenith of their fame – thus we see the oak when a plant
annoyed & cropt by the ass & even the sheep & trampled
under foot by the meanest of the forrest that when a tree

despises such petty insults & leaves them at his feet & even dares the four winds of heaven into turbulance & remains flourishing in vigour & beauty true courage is a great honour & the actions of the brave are engrafted with the eternitys of posterity on the laurels of the muses of verse & history as deeds that cannot die 'Let the bravest follow me' was the danger daring war cry of Marat[11] one of the heroes of the Napoleon Dynasty & it will be rememberd among the soul stirring honours of heroes when the history of france that records it become as old in antiquity as the deeds of an Alexander & the pomp & splendour of a Darius – but every species of courage is not honour thus the butchers dog cannot be denied courage when it attacks the infuriated bull but it is brute courage & not alied to honour would that brute courage were confined to brutes only but we often see it exercised by man & what is worse by man considered honourable

    Strange deeds but what of that
    The most dishonest seem the most approved

& brute courage is often employed in the extention of empire which is falsely entitled the honours of victory but these consequences are made up of two ingredients the follys of expensive splendour & the evils of excessive crueltys & oppressions & the greatest achievements of the greatest ty-rants are found in two words ambition & power which un-luckily for the actor in such dramas neither means happiness or eternity – yet although reason tells us that all honours are the attributes of good & meritorious actions when we hear it fashionably discussed in fashionable company we are puz-zled to make out what their ideas of honour are further then the attendants of pride possesion & power & more astonished to discover the ways & means by which such honours are attained but we must not over shoot our reason so far as to fancy that honour makes distinctions between man & man but in man & actions pride sees agrement & a degrading difference between the pewter badge of a workhouse & the silver star of a court but reason only marks it in the metal for what difference can there be in the men if their situations only denote it for why is the poor honest dependant on a workhouse less honourable than the dependant on a court is it beggarly to be beholden for a few shillings weekly to the parish which every little hamlet is called & honourable to be penshioned for thousands a year on the overburthened parish of the country where is the honour or where is the beggary – Alexander that most illustrious & most extravagant of noble paupers who rated the whole world into a parish & drained it to the lees for a maintenance to support his tyranny & his honour stands now but as a pigmy beside that atlas of fame & poverty Homer who shared the common lot of a beggar wandering from door to door reciteing his poems to win a trifle from charity to support his existance – time alone gave him his universal honours unsolicited the only thing which Alexander solicited & was denied of for his heroic actions are divided with his cruel usurpations & like the blights of winter & the blooms of summer they live on together in sunshine & shadow & not the unsullied splendour & sunshine of fame – Honour creates or stirs up many phantasys & abides in many shapes in the many stages & associations of the human mind & every constitution warms with its constitutional emulation to gratification thus with the clown honour sits in a holiday suit of cloaths – with the gentleman it is in great fortunes with the lady it triumphs as beauty with the author as fame with generals as conquests & victory with kings as empire – would it were considered by all & every one that to make honour consistant truth as well as opinion there is only [one] thing always nessesary & that is honesty – for the commonest honesty is a grand principle that confers greatness to a king & honour to poverty 'The world' saith Dr Knox[12] 'abounds with evil moral natural real & imaginary. He alone who does all he can wherever his influence extends to mortgage & remove is the true nobleman others are Earls Marquises Dukes & Kings'

The Journey from Essex

July 24th 1841   Returned home out of Essex & found no
Mary – her & her family are as nothing to me now though
she herself was once the dearest of all – & how can I forget

Journal July 18—1841—Sunday—Felt very melancholly –
went a walk on the forest[1] in the afternoon – fell in with
some gipseys one of whom offered to assist in my escape
from the mad house by hideing me in his camp to which I
almost agreed but told him I had no money to start with but
if he would do so I would promise him fifty pounds & he
agreed to do so before saturday on friday I went again but
he did not seem so willing so I said little about it – on Sunday
I went & they were all gone – I found[2] an old wide awake
hat & an old straw bonnet of the plumb pudding sort was
left behind – & I put the hat in my pocket thinking it might
be usefull for another oppertunity & as good luck would
have it, it turned out to be so
July 19 Monday   Did nothing
July 20   Reconnitred the rout the gipsey pointed out &
found it a legible one to make a movement & having only
honest courage & myself in my army I Led the way & my
troops soon followed but being careless in mapping down
the rout as the Gipsey told me I missed the lane to Enfield
town & was going down Enfield highway till I passed 'The
Labour in vain' Public house where a person I knew comeing
out of the door told me the way
   I walked down the lane gently & was soon in Enfield
Town & bye & bye on the great York Road where it was all
plain sailing & stearing ahead meeting no enemy & fearing

none I reached Stevenage where being Night I got over a gate crossed over the corner of a green paddock where seeing a pond or hollow in the corner I forced to stay off a respectable distance to keep from falling into it for my legs were nearly knocked up & began to stagger I scaled some old rotten paleings into the yard & then had higher pailings to clamber over to get into the shed or hovel which I did with difficulty being rather weak & to my good luck I found some trusses of clover piled up about 6 or more feet square which I gladly mounted & slept on there was some trays in the hovel on which I could have reposed had I not found a better bed I slept soundly but had a very uneasy dream I thought my first wife lay on my left arm & somebody took her away from my side – which made me wake up rather unhappy I thought as I awoke somebody said 'Mary' but nobody was near – I lay down with my head towards the north to show myself the steering point in the morning

July 21 Daylight was looking in on every side & fearing my garrison might be taken by storm & myself be made prisoner I left my lodging by the way I got in & thanked God for his kindness in procureing it (for anything in a famine is better then nothing & any place that giveth the weary rest is a blessing) I gained the north road again & steered due north – on the left hand side the road under the bank like a cave I saw a Man & boy coiled up asleep which I hailed & they woke up to tell me the name of the next village[3] Some where on the London side the 'Plough' Public house a Man passed me on horseback in a Slop frock & said 'here's another of the broken down haymakers' & threw me a penny to get a half pint of beer which I picked up & thanked him for & when I got to the plough I called for a half pint & drank it & got a rest & escaped a very heavy shower in the bargain by having a shelter till it was over – afterwards I would have begged a penny of two drovers who were very saucey so I begged no more of any body meet who I would

I passed 3 or 4 good built houses on a hill & a public house on the road side in the hollow below them I seemed to pass the Milestones very quick in the morning – but toward night they seemed to be stretched further asunder I

[118]

got to a village further on & forgot the name the road on the left hand was quite over shaded by some tree & quite dry so I sat down half an hour & made a good many wishes for breakfast but wishes was no hearty meal so I got up as hungry as I sat down – I forget here the names of the villages I passed through but reccolect at late evening going through Potton in Bedfordshire where I called in a house to light my pipe in which was a civil old woman & a young country wench makeing lace on a cushion as round as a globe & a young fellow all civil people – I asked them a few questions as to the way & where the clergyman & overseer lived but they scarcely heard me or gave me no answer[4] I then went through Potton & happened with a kind talking countryman who told me the Parson lived a good way from where I was or overseer I do'n't know which so I went on hopping with a crippled foot for the gravel had got into my old shoes one of which had now nearly lost the sole Had I found the overseers house at hand or the Parsons I should have gave my name & begged for a shilling to carry me home but I was forced to brush on pennyless & be thankfull I had a leg to move on – I then asked him wether he could tell me of a farm yard any where on the road where I could find a shed & some dry straw & he said yes & if you will go with me I will show you the place – its a public house on the left hand side of the road at the sign of the 'Ram' but seeing a stone or flint heap[5] I longed to rest as one of my feet was very painfull so I thanked him for his kindness & bid him go on – but the good natured fellow lingered awhile as if wishing to conduct me & then suddenly recolecting that he had a hamper on his shoulder & a lock up bag in his hand cramfull to meet the coach which he feared missing – he started hastily & was soon out of sight – I followed looking in vain for the countrymans straw bed & not being able to meet it I lay down by a shed side under some Elm trees between the wall & the trees being a thick row planted some 5 or 6 feet from the buildings I lay there & tried to sleep but the wind came in between them so cold that I lay till I quaked like the ague & quitted the lodging for a better at the Ram which I could hardly hope to find – It now began to grow dark apace & the odd houses on the road began to light up & show the

[119]

This old house, over a mile from Potton on the road to Gamlingay Great Heath, can almost certainly be identified as Clare's 'Ram'. It was a public house within living memory and is

(Photograph by John Baguley)

inside tennants lots very comfortable & my outside lot very uncomfortable & wretched – still I hobbled forward as well as I could & at last came to the Ram the shutters were not closed & the lighted window looked very cheering but I had no money & did not like to go in there was a sort of shed or gighouse at the end but I did not like to lie there as the people were up – so I still travelled on the road was very lonely & dark in places being overshaded with trees at length I came to a place where the road branched off into two turnpikes one to the right about & the other straight forward & on going bye my eye glanced on a mile stone standing under the hedge so I heedlessly turned back to read it to see where the other road led too & on doing so I found it led to London I then suddenly forgot which was North or South & though I narrowly examined both ways I could see no tree or bush or stone heap that I could reccolect I had passed so I went on mile after mile almost convinced I was going the same way I came & these thoughts were so strong upon me that doubt & hopelessnes made me turn so feeble that I was scarcely able to walk yet I could not sit down or give up but shuffled along till I saw a lamp shining as bright as the moon which on nearing I found was suspended over a Tollgate before I got through the man came out with a candle & eyed me narrowly but having no fear I stopt to ask him wether I was going northward & he said when you get through the gate you are; so I thanked him kindly & went through on the other side & gathered my old strength as my doubts vanished I soon cheered up & hummed the air of highland Mary as I went on I at length fell in with an odd house all alone near a wood but I could not see what the sign was though the sign seemed to stand oddly enough in a sort of trough or spout there was a large porch over the door & being weary I crept in & glad enough I was to find I could lye with my legs straight the inmates were all gone to roost for I could hear them turn over in bed as I lay at full length on the stones in the poach [porch] – I slept here till daylight & felt very much refreshed as I got up – I blest my two wives & both their familys when I lay down & when I got up & when I thought of some former difficultys on a like occasion I could not help blessing the Queen

[121]

Having passed a Lodge on the left hand within a mile & a half or less of a town I think it might be St Ives[6] but I forget the name I sat down to rest on a flint heap[7] where I might rest half an hour or more & while sitting here I saw a tall Gipsey come out of the Lodge gate & make down the road towards where I was sitting when she got up to me on seeing she was a young woman with an honest looking countenance rather handsome I spoke to her & asked her a few questions which she answered readily & with evident good humour so I got up and went on to the next town with her – she cautioned me on the way to put somthing in my hat to keep the crown up & said in a lower tone 'you'll be noticed' but not knowing what she hinted – I took no notice & made no reply At length she pointed to a small tower church which she called Shefford Church & advised me to go on a footway which would take me direct to it & I should shorten my journey fifteen miles by doing so I would gladly have taken the young woman's advice feeling that it was honest & a nigh guess towards the truth but fearing I might loose my way & not be able to find the north road again I thanked her & told her I should keep to the road when she bade me 'good day' & went into a house or shop on the left hand side of the road[8]

I have but a slight reccolection of my journey between here & Stilton for I was knocked up & noticed little or nothing one night I lay in a dyke bottom from the wind & went sleep[9] half an hour when I suddenly awoke & found one side wet through from the sock[10] in the dyke bottom so I got out & went on – I remember going down a very dark road hung over with trees on both sides very thick which seemed to extend a mile or two I then entered a town & some of the chamber windows had candle lights shineing in them – I felt so weary here that I forced to sit down on the ground to rest myself & while I sat here a Coach[11] that seemed to be heavy laden came rattling up & stopt in the hollow below me & I cannot reccolect its ever passing by me I then got up & pushed onward seeing little to notice for the road very often looked as stupid as myself & I was very often half asleep as I went on the third day I satisfied my hunger by eating the grass by the road side which seemed to taste something like bread I was hungry & eat heartily till I was satisfied & in fact the meal seemed to do me good the next and last day I reccolected that I had some tobacco & my box of lucifers being exhausted I could not light my pipe so I took to chewing Tobacco all day & eat the quids when I had done & I was never hungry afterwards – I remember passing through Buckden & going a length of road afterwards but I dont reccolect the name of any place untill I came to Stilton where I was compleatly foot foundered & broken down when I had got about half way through the town a gravel causeway invited me to rest myself so I lay down & nearly went sleep a young woman (so I guessed by the voice) came out of a house & said 'poor creature' & another more elderly said 'O he shams' but when I got up the latter said 'O no he don't' as I hobbled along very lame I heard the voices but never looked back to see where they came from – when I got near the Inn at the end of the gravel walk I maet [met] two young women & I asked one of them wether the road branching to the right bye the end of the Inn did not lead to Peterborough & she said 'Yes' it did so as soon as ever I was on it I felt myself in homes way & went on rather more cheerfull & though I forced to rest oftener than usual before I got to Peterborough a man & woman passed me in a cart & on hailing me as they passed I found they were neighbours from Helpstone where I used to live – I told them I was knocked up which they could easily see & that I had neither eat or drank any thing since I left Essex when I told my story they clubbed together & threw me fivepence out of the cart I picked it up & called at a small public house near the bridge were I had two half pints of ale & two-penn'o'th of bread & cheese when I had done I started quite refreshed only my feet was more crippled then ever & I could scarcely make a walk of it over the stones & being half ashamed to sit down in the street I forced to keep on the move & got through Peterborough better than I expected when I got on the high road I rested on the stone heaps as I passed till I was able to go on afresh & bye & bye I passed Walton & soon reached Werrington I was making for the Beehive as fast as I could when a cart met me with a man & woman & a boy in it when nearing me the woman jumped out & caught fast hold of my

[123]

hands & wished me to get into the cart but I refused & thought her either drunk or mad but when I was told it was my second wife Patty I got in & was soon at Northborough but Mary was not there neither could I get any information about her further then the[12] old story of her being dead six years ago which might be taken from a bran new old Newspaper printed a dozen years ago but I took no notice of the blarney having seen her myself about a twelvemonth ago alive & well & as young as ever – so here I am homeless at home & half gratified to feel that I can be happy anywhere

> May none those marks of my sad fate efface
> For they appeal from tyranny to God
>   Byron

To Mary Clare – Glinton
                              Northborough July 27 1841
My dear wife
        I have written an account of my journey or rather escape from Essex for your amusement & hope it may divert [?] your leisure hours – I would have told you before now that I got here to Northborough last friday night but not being able to see you or hear where you was I soon began to feel homeless at home & shall bye & bye feel nearly hopeless but not so lonely as I did in Essex – for here I can see Glinton Church & feeling that Mary is safe if not happy I am gratified[13] though my home is no home to me my hopes are not entirely hopeless while even the memory of Mary lives so near me God bless you My dear Mary – give my love to your dear & beautifull family & to your Mother – & believe me as I ever have been & ever shall be
                My dearest Mary
                    Your affectionate Husband
                         John Clare

Notes

Introduction

1 Now Helpston. See *Sketches in the life of John Clare by himself*, edited by Edmund Blunden, pp. 45, 46.

2 *Sketches in the life of John Clare by himself.*

3 ibid.

4 See *The Prose of John Clare*, edited by J. W. and Anne Tibble, p. 13.

5 James Thomson, *The Seasons* (1726–30).

6 Letter to John Taylor, *The Letters of John Clare*, edited by J. W. and Anne Tibble, p. 132.

7 *PN Review* 6, 1.

8 By William Hilton, RA, 1820, now in the National Portrait Gallery.

9 *Sketches in the life of John Clare by himself*, p. 120.

10 *London Magazine*, August 1824.

11 By J. L. and Barbara Hammond (Longmans 1911).

12 See *European Magazine*, November 1825; also J. L. Cherry, *John Clare: life and remains* (1873), p. 308.

13 *The Letters of John Clare*, pp. 304, 305.

14 See Essay on Landscape in *The Prose of John Clare*, p. 213.

15 See *The Poetical Works of Samuel Taylor Coleridge*, edited by William B. Scott (Routledge), p. 144 and note.

16 *The Poems of John Clare*, edited by J. W. Tibble, vol. 2.

17 Introduction to *John Clare: poems chiefly from manuscript*, edited by Edmund Blunden.

18 *The Later Poems of John Clare*, edited by Eric Robinson and Geoffrey Summerfield, has 'Poh'. The reading is problematic.

19 Stanzas for this poem are in the Northampton MSS 6, 7 and 8; the Peterborough MSS 49 and 57; and the Bodleian MSS Don a 8 and Don C 64. For variant versions see *Poems of John Clare's*

Madness, edited by Geoffrey Grigson; *The Later Poems of John Clare*, edited by Eric Robinson and Geoffrey Summerfield; and for complete seasonal form, *Selected Poems*, edited by J. W. and Anne Tibble.

20 'Written in a thunder storm, 15 July 1841', *The Poems of John Clare*, vol. 2, p. 391.

21 *Selected Poems*, Everyman edition, pp. 311–12.

22 Northampton MSS.

23 'Love's Story', *Selected Poems*, Everyman edition, pp. 313–14.

24 'I hid my love': Knight's transcripts, Northampton MSS, have *buss* (kiss); Edmund Blunden (1920) and Geoffrey Grigson (1950) read *bass*; Eric Robinson and Geoffrey Summerfield give Knight's *buss* and as meanings, kiss, and a variant of buzz. It is likely that Clare wrote *buzz* and that Knight mistook his customary way of writing zz for ss.

25 *rauk* (also spelt *rawk* by Clare) is a thick East Anglian fog: O.E. *roke*.

26 The Northampton MS has the title 'Spring'.

The Journal

1 Francis Moore, astrologer and quack physician, began in 1699 to publish an almanac to advertise his pills. Imitations continue to this day to be published annually.

2 John Foxe (1516–87), *Actes and Monuments of these latter perilous times touching matters of the Church*, popularly known as *Foxe's Book of Martyrs*. Clare's copy was given him by his father.

3 Clare's love of Izaak Walton's *The Compleat Angler* (1653) continued; see letter of February 1848 in *The Letters of John Clare* (1951).

4 The letter to Allan Cunningham has not, as far as I know, survived; the other was to H. F. Cary (1772–1844), translator of Dante. Clare asked Cary to follow his article in the *London Magazine* with one on Robert Bloomfield (see notes 40 and 41 below).

5 Eight Natural History Letters – and some 'Nature Notes' – are included in *The Prose of John Clare* (1951). Three of the Letters are in America.

6 Charles Abraham Elton, author of *The Brothers, a monody* (1820) and *Boyhood: with Other Poems and Translations* (1835). Elton has not received due recognition.

7 One of Charles Lamb's *Essays of Elia* (1823), of which the first series appeared in the *London Magazine*, 1820–23.

8 A refutation of Goethe's claim to a place beside Homer and Shakespeare.

9 Thomas Chatterton (1752–70).

10 See the Appendices at the end of the Journal.

11 The authorship of Horace Walpole's novel *The Castle of Otranto* (1764) was not acknowledged until a second edition was called for within a year. The first edition purported to be the translation of an Italian manuscript of 1529.

12 The original is among the Clare MSS at Northampton. See note on Appendices.

13 The redcap, goldfinch, *Carduelis elegans*.

14 Head gardener at Milton Hall. See J. W. and Anne Tibble, *John Clare: a Life* (1932), p. 116.

15 Byron's epic satire (1819–24).

16 Harry Stoe Van Dyk; for his help to Clare over publication of *The Shepherd's Calendar*, see *John Clare: a life*, pp. 214, 215, 217, 274–5, 302.

17 James Augustus Hessey, partner of John Taylor, Clare's publisher.

18 Old Testament.

19 Half-yearly hiring day for agricultural workers. See 'Help-stone Statute' in *The Poems of John Clare* (1935).

20 Unpublished.

21 William Collins (1721–59), best known for his *Odes* (1757).

22 Thomas Gray (1716–71). In his library Clare had copies of Gray's *Poetical Works* (1809), *Poetical Works* (1826) and Gray's *Letters* (1819).

23 John Ogilvie (1733–1813) wrote *The Day of Judgment* (1753), *Rona* (1777), *Britannia*, a national epic poem in twenty books (1801), and much other verse.

24 Clare possessed copies of the *Works* (1814) and the *Poetical Works* (1817) of Robert Burns.

25 An anonymous collection of short tales (1824).

26 The vicar of Helpstone.

27 Archaeologist friend of Clare's, employed as butler at Milton; author of *Durobrivae*.

28 Taylor and Hessey published Josiah Conder's poems, *The Star in the East* (1824). Conder was editor of the *Eclectic Review*.

29 *The Garden of Florence and other poems* (1821) by John Hamilton Reynolds (1796–1852).

30 Clare's underlining.

31 'The sleeping children' in Lichfield Cathedral.

32 See note on Appendices.

33 I have failed so far to identify 'Surry', or 'Surrey'.

34 An unidentified school book.

35 *Remarks on the Internal Evidence for the Truth of Revealed Religion* (1820). Thomas Erskine wrote many other theological works.

36 Appendix 5 is printed in this volume, see p. 86

37 Richard Savage (d. 1793).

38 Samuel Johnson's *Lives of the Poets* (1779–81).

39 'Or the Groans of Samuel Sensitive and Timothy Testy, with a few supplementary sighs from Mrs Testy' (1801), anon.

40 Robert Bloomfield (1766–1823), author of *The Farmer's Boy* (1800), of which 26,000 are said to have been sold in three years.

41 Joseph Weston (not Preston) edited *The Remains of Robert Bloomfield* (1825). See also Journal entries for 5 and 8 March 1825.

42 Capel Lofft, a Suffolk squire with whose help Bloomfield's *The Farmer's Boy* was published in 1800. In *English Bards and Scotch Reviewers* (1809) Byron wrote of 'distressed versemen'.

43 A novel attributed to Sir Walter Scott but actually written by G. W. Haering. See also note 109.

44 Robert Tannahill (1777–1810), a Paisley weaver, published *Poems and Songs* in 1815. For a time his songs were second only in popularity to those of Burns.

45 The wife of Clare's friend Octavius Gilchrist.

46 Charles Lloyd, a young friend of Lamb's.

47 John Banton; *The Village Wreath* (1822) and *Excursions of Fancy* (1824) are both in Clare's library at Northampton.

48 S. Messing; *Rural Walks* (1819) and *Poems on Various Subjects* (1821) are also in Clare's library. Rose, Wilkinson and Stratton I have not been able to trace.

49 Anna Adcock, *Cottage Poems* (1808).

50 William Hazlitt, *Lectures on the English Poets* (1818–19).

51 *English Comic Writers* (1819).

52 *Characters of Shakespeare's Plays* (1817–18).

53 Hugh Blair (1718–1800), *Sermons*, 5 vols, (1777–1801).

54 James Maddock, *The Florist's Directory* (1822).

55 John Taylor had recently published *Flora Domestica, or the portable flower garden* (1823) by Leigh Hunt's sister-on-law, Elizabeth Kent. Clare's letters to her have not yet come to light.

56 Alexander Pope, *An Essay on Man* (1733–4). The Pastorals were entitled *Windsor Forest* (1713).

57 Clare saw beyond the 'Dulness' which earned Hill a place in Pope's satire *The Dunciad* (1728).

58 See the Appendices.

59 *Essays Moral and Literary* (1778) by Vicesimus Knox (1752–1821). See Clare's letter to Octavius Gilchrist of September 1820 in *The Letters of John Clare* (1951); Clare had already received a copy of the *Essays* (1819) from Lord Radstock.

60 *Of Gardens*. The 1815 and the 1819 editions are both in Clare's library.

61 'The Waterfall and the Eglantine' – Clare's slip.

62 Possibly *The Life of God in the Soul of Man* (1821) by Henry Scougal. These 'two Volumes of Sermons' mentioned by Clare are not distinguishable among the many books given him by Lord Radstock and now in his library at Northampton.

63 Herb Paris, 'true love', *Paris quadrifolia*, can no longer be found in Oxey Wood, or fly orchises in Harrison's pailgrounds, or spider orchises anywhere in Clare country, as far as I know. But in 1978 bee and butterfly orchises, moth mullein and yellow water-lilies were growing where Clare found them. For further mention of orchises and mullein, see the Natural History Letters printed in *The Prose of John Clare* (1951), p. 163.

64 Hugh Blair, *Sermons* (1819).

65 Shady. See Anne Elizabeth Baker, *Glossary of Northamptonshire Words and Phrases* (1854), with which Clare helped.

66 *Clematis Vitalba*, traveller's joy, wild clematis.

67 John Scott, editor of the *London Magazine* before Clare's publisher, John Taylor. Scott was killed in a duel in 1821.

68 Thomas Percy (1729–1811), Bishop of Dromore, published *Reliques of Ancient English Poetry* in 1765.

69 Brushwood, low bushes in wood or forest.

70 Thomas Inskip championed Bloomfield. Later he visited Clare in St Andrew's asylum, Northampton. He published five or more of Clare's poems written at St Andrews, in the Bedford Times during the 1840s.

71 James Thomson (1700–48), *The Seasons* (1726–30).

72 Thomas Tusser (1524?–80), author of *Hundreth good pointes of husbandrie* (1557), a collection of instructions in verse on farming, gardening and housekeeping. Clare's edition was *Five Hundred Points of Good Husbandry* (1812).

73 William Fordyce Mavor (1768–1837), compiler of educational works.

74 From the verb 'to straddle' (1574), to measure by a man's strides the width needed for a stack.

75 Empty shells of the banded snail.

76 Young swallows which miss migration normally die during the winter.

77 Robert Southey, *Life of Wesley* (1820).

78 Connected with 'straum', 'strime', 'strome'. Clare is using the past tense, 'strum', here, meaning measured with yard-long strides.

79 *The Death of Abel*, in five books (1814) by Salomon Gessner (1730–88). Translated into English it was for a time popular.

80 See the Appendices.

81 *The Human Heart* (1824) in Clare's library at Northampton is anonymous.

82 See Journal entry for 20 August 1825.

83 See note 1.

84 Appendix 9 is given in full on p. 88.

85 Long-tailed titmouse (*Acredula candata*), see James Fisher, *The Birds of John Clare* (1956).

86 See note 55.

87 W. Sharpe of the Dead Letter Office. Later Sharpe gave useful service to Clare by collecting payments from London publishers of Annuals (popular Christmas books).

88 Clare sent 'The Vanitys of Life' to Montgomery, editor of the *Sheffield Iris*, who printed it in the paper in 1825. See *John Clare: a life*, pp. 279 and 280, for information about Clare's poems written 'in the manner of the oldern Poets'; also notes 129 and 134 below. 'The Vanitys of Life' was reprinted in *The Rural Muse* and in *Ancient Ballads and Songs of the Peasantry of England* (1851). See *Notes and Queries* (1873) for affirmation of the poem's authenticity.

89 The brown beetle of early summer, with leaf-like antennae, is the cockchafer. Here Clare must mean the 'shardborne' black dorbeetle.

90 See note 21.

91 Possibly *Sorbus torminalis*.

92 John Parkinson, *Theatrum botanicum* (1640).

93 See note 43.

94 Robert Montgomery (1807–55), author of religious poems and editor of the *Sheffield Iris*. See also note 88.

95 From his descriptions Clare seems to have in mind the bird usually called the mistle, or missel, thrush. 'Mavis' is the name given to the smaller song-thrush, which has a song and builds a nest quite different from those of the missel thrush.

96 See note 41.

97 See note 55.

98 William Dodd (1729–77), a forger who, according to Horace Walpole, nevertheless preached 'very eloquently and touchingly'. While under sentence of death Dodd wrote *Thoughts in Prison* (1777).

99 The Old Testament, Micah 7:8–10. 'Rejoice not against me, O mine enemy: when I fall, I shall arise; when I sit in darkness, the Lord shall be a light unto me.

'I will bear the indignation of the Lord, because I have sinned against him, until he plead my cause, and execute judgment for me; he will bring me forth to the light, and I shall behold his righteousness.

'Then she that is mine enemy shall see it, and shame shall cover her which said unto me, Where is the Lord thy God? mine eyes shall behold her: now shall she be trodden down as the mire of the streets.'

100 The 'Natural History of Helpstone' was never completed. Eight of Clare's Natural History letters, lists of birds and orchises and some fragmentary notes, are printed in *The Prose of John Clare* (1951).

101 John Taylor had handed over to Henry Southern the editing of the *London Magazine* in a last effort to revive that once flourishing monthly.

102 Anna Laetitia Barbauld's *Lessons for Children from Two to Three Years Old* (1779).

103 Hannah More (1745–1853) wrote this on her deathbed. She belonged to the Blue Stocking coterie and knew Dr Johnson.

104 Thomas Wilson (1663–1755), Bishop of Sodor and Man, wrote *Maxims of Piety and Christianity* (1789) and other devotional manuals.

105 Gilbert Burnet (1643–1715), Bishop of Salisbury, had broad views on politics and religion; he wrote a Preface to Henry Scougal's *The Life of God in the Soul of Man, or The Nature and Excellency of the Christian Religion, with the method of attaining the Happiness it possesses* (1677).

106 Richard Watson (1737–1816), Bishop of Llandaff, wrote *An Apology for the Bible* (1796) in a series of letters addressed to Thomas Paine. This answer to the 'low blackguard' was read in America as well as in Britain.

107 William Hone (1780–1842) edited the *Every-day Book* (1826–7). There is a copy in Clare's library. See also note 129 below.

108 *The Scientific Receptacle* (1825) is also in Clare's library.

Seven of Clare's poems written 'in the manner of the olden Poets' were published in this edition. See *John Clare: a life*, pp. 278, 307, 308.

109 Clare's edition of *Walladmor* is 'freely translated into German from the English of Sir Walter Scott, and now freely translated from the German into English' by Thomas De Quincey (Taylor & Hessey 1825). See also note 43.

110 Charles Vyse, *The Tutor's Guide: being a complete System of Arithmetic; with various branches of the Mathematics* (1770).

111 Even in Clare's day snake's-head fritillary was only to be found in certain areas; it is now very rare.

112 Redpoll, *Acanthis linaria*, or *Acanthis rufescens*.

113 From the entry for 10 May 1825 it is clear that Clare identified the chiff-chaff, his 'Pettichap or hoverbird', among the warblers. But from his important group of poems on birds and their nests, *Poems*, (1935) vol. 2, and *The Midsummer Cushion* (1979) pp. 387–489 *passim*, it is just as clear that the 'Pettichap's nest' he describes so exactly, is in fact the nest of a willow-warbler. In *The Natural History and Antiquities of Selborne* (1789) Gilbert White described the chiff-chaff as the 'smallest willow-wren'; the willow-warbler as the 'middle willow-wren'; and the wood-warbler as the 'largest willow-wren'.

114 In *Notes on the Birds of Northamptonshire and Neighbourhood* (1895) Lord Lilford writes that the grasshopper warbler was 'formerly very abundant' in the Fens. This was Clare's 'cricket bird' – see Journal entry for 6 May 1825.

115 Clare was right. The reason for the migration of this species between the south of England and Scotland is still unknown.

116 In answer to the words of his publisher, John Taylor, 'Better to terminate the connection than continue it in Distrust', Clare had written: 'I have no desire to seek another publisher, neither do I believe any other woud do as well for me as you may do much less better.' (*The Letters of John Clare*, p. 170).

117 The grasshopper warbler, *Locustella naevia*, extinct now in Clare country. See note 114.

118 The hobby falcon, *Falco subbutco*.

119 The chiff-chaff, *Phylloscopus rufus*.

120 Elizabeth Kent's 'History of Birds', intended as a companion volume to her *Flora Domestica* (see note 55) and *Sylvan Sketches*, was not in fact completed.

121 Edward Irving, founder of the Scottish religious sect, the Irvingites.

122 Thomas Nugent (1700?–72), *Travels through Germany . . . in a series of letters to a friend* (1768), 2 vols.

123 Clare's list of local orchises is in the Peterborough MSS.

124 Broom-rape, *Orobanche major*. This is not an orchis.

125 In a list of 'orchis's counted from privet hedges' (now in the Northampton Clare Collection) Clare makes no mention of 'white piegon' (his usual spelling of pigeon) orchis.

126 The independent views expressed in 'Struggles of a Senior Wrangler' attracted Clare's sympathy. The *London Magazine* of June 1825 also included 'The Wedding' by Elia – see note 7 above.

127 *The Shepherd's Calendar* (1827) contained (almost half its contents) 'Village Stories'. 'The Sorrows of Love' was the first of these four long tales. They are not in *The Poems of John Clare* (1935) nor were they reprinted in the 1964 edition of *The Shepherd's Calendar*, edited by Eric Robinson and Geoffrey Summerfield.

128 Richard Ayton, *Essays and Sketches of Character* (1825).

129 See note 107. 'Death', the poem 'fatherd on Andrew Marvel', was published in Hone's *Every-Day Book*, June 1825. See also Journal entry for 2 July 1825.

130 See note 87.

131 Probably the common, or corn, bunting, *Emberiza miliaria*.

132 He was 32.

133 John Taylor and Clare did not see eye to eye about the kind of poetry Clare was writing in 1825, or the kind he wished to write. When Taylor had recovered from an attack of brain fever he defended himself against Clare's complaints about delay over publication of *The Shepherd's Calendar* by writing: 'The poems are not only slovenly written, but as slovenly composed.' Clare set about rewriting much of *The Shepherd's Calendar*.

134 Sir John Harington (or Harrington) (1561–1612). Hone did not accept the poem 'A Farewell and Defiance to Love', 'fatherd' on Harington and signed 'Frederick Roberts of Milton'. The poem was printed in the *European Magazine* (1825). See *John Clare: a life*, pp. 277–80.

135 See note 108.

136 Barron Field planned to write a life of his friend Charles Lamb, and another of William Wordsworth – who dissuaded him. Nor did Field in fact edit Octavius Gilchrist's papers.

137 Robert Bloomfield (note 40), *Hazelwood Hall* (1823), a village drama in three acts.

138 Now unknown.

139 For correspondence with Alaric A. Watts, J. Power and W. Baynes, see *John Clare: Letters*.

'First Love's Reccolections' – not the first of the many Mary Joyce poems – was printed in *The Rural Muse* (1835).

140 'Broomsgrove' was set to music. See *John Clare: a life*, p. 264.

APPENDIX 5

1 *The Shepherd's Calendar* came out in 1827. Clare had been trying since 1822 to comply with John Taylor's directions for his poems.

2 *Poems Descriptive of Rural Life and Scenery*, 1820; four editions appeared within the year. *The Village Minstrel*, 1821, sold poorly.

3 Octavius Gilchrist died in 1823. He was a trusted friend.

APPENDIX 9

1 Clare's usual name for the village, in this case Helpstone.
2 paddock.
3 meteor.
4 distorted.
5 Clare could intend *yawning*, or he could mean *yawing* – hanging unsteadily above.

The Essays

1 Clearly one of the seventeen species of 'bumble', *Bombus terrestris*, which make nests of moss in the ground.
2 Gap in MS: *desisted*?
3 *stature*?
4 *Raphael*?
5 *exquisite*?
6 *chef d'oeuvre*
7 gap of one word in MS.
8 A military commander; formerly written *Bashaw* now *Pasha*

9 *were*

10 Epaminondas, a Theban general of the 4th century BC.

11 Jean-Paul Marat, writer and politician of the French Revolution, assassinated in 1793.

12 John Knox, champion of the Reformation in Scotland. Died 1572.

The Journey from Essex

1 Epping.

2 Clare has crossed out 'I found'.

3 Clare's note: 'Baldeck', i.e., Baldock. Here Clare has inserted + + and at the end of the disjointed MS are the words to be inserted: 'Somewhere . . . meet who I would'.

4 At the foot of the page, under Baldeck, Clare wrote: 'This note should be placed at the bottom of the page

+ Note On searching my pockets after the above was written I found part of a newspaper vide 'Morning Chronicle' on which the following fragments were pencilled soon after I got the information from labourers going to work or travellers journying along to better their condition as I was hopeing to do mine in fact I believed I saw home in every ones countenance which seemed so cheerfull in my own – 'There is no place like home' the following was written by the Road side 1st Day – Tuesday started from Enfield & slept at Stevenage on some clover trusses – cold lodging

Wednesday – Jacks Hill is passed already consisting of a beer shop & some houses on the hill appearing newly built – the last Mile stone 35 Miles from London got through Baldeck & sat under a dry hedge & had a rest in lieu of breakfast Text continued'

5 See note 7.

6 Clare's note: 'It was St Neots'

7 Either the 'stone or flint heap' Clare has mentioned (note 5) or this 'flint heap' must be where, in a small notebook he had with him on the journey, he wrote:

'The man whose daughter is the Queen of England is now sitting on a stone heap on the highway to bugden [Buckden] without a farthing in his pocket & without eating a bit of food ever since yesterday morning – when he was offered a bit of Bread & cheese at Enfield – he has not had any since but if I put a little fresh speed on hope too may speed tomorrow – O Mary mary If you knew

[135]

how anxious I am to see you & dear Patty with the children I think
you would come & meet me'

8 Clare has marked two passages thus + + on a later page in
the octavo manuscript – MS 6 at Northampton – under 'Reccolections &c of Journey from Essex – Placed at the end of the Journey
& apart from it', but there is no indication in the text as to where
the second passage – 'Having passed a Lodge . . . left hand side
the road' should go. He was, on his own evidence, 'very weary'
between Potton and Stilton, perhaps from as far south as Shefford,
so that the place of the passage, like the whereabouts of the 'flint
heap' and the 'stone or flint heap' cannot with certainty be
identified.

9 'went sleep', like 'went bed', are common expressions in the
East Midlands.

10 From the verb to sog, to soak through. See Anne Elizabeth
Baker, *Glossary of Northamptonshire Words and Phrases* (1854)
with which Clare had helped.

11 Clare's note + at the foot of the page (MS 6): 'The coach did
pass me as I sat under some trees by a high wall & the lamps
flashed in my face & wakened me up from a doze when I knocked
the gravel out of my shoes & started'.

12 Clare has crossed out one word: ? new.

13 Clare has crossed out 'to believe I shall be the same'.

Bibliography

JOHN CLARE'S WORKS

Poems Descriptive of Rural Life and Scenery, printed for Taylor & Hessey, and E. Drury (London 1820; second and third editions 1820; fourth edition 1821).

The Village Minstrel, and Other Poems, printed for Taylor & Hessey, and E. Drury, 2 vols (London 1821; second edition 1823).

The Shepherd's Calendar; with Village Stories, and Other Poems (published for John Taylor by James Duncan, London 1827).

Sketches in the life of John Clare by himself, with an Introduction, Notes and additions by Edmund Blunden (Cobden Sanderson 1931).

The Midsummer Cushion, written c. 1830. Fair copy prepared by John Clare edited by Anne Tibble with R. K. R. Thornton as associate editor (published for the first time by Mid Northumberland Arts Group in association with Carcanet Press 1979).

BIOGRAPHIES

The Life of John Clare by Frederick Martin (Macmillan 1865).

The Life and Remains of John Clare by J. L. Cherry, illustrated by Birket Foster (Frederick Warne; J. Taylor & Son, Northampton, 1873).

John Clare: a life by J. W. and Anne Tibble (Cobden-Sanderson 1932).

John Clare: his life and poetry by J. W. and Anne Tibble (Heinemann 1956).

LETTERS

The Letters of John Clare edited by J. W. and Anne Tibble (Routledge & Kegan Paul 1951).

POETRY AND PROSE

Poems by John Clare selected and introduced by Norman Gale, with a bibliography by C. Ernest Smith (George E. Over, Rugby, 1901).

Poems by John Clare edited, with an introduction, by Arthur Symons (Henry Frowde 1908).

Madrigals and Chronicles: being newly found poems written by John Clare edited, with a preface and commentary, by Edmund Blunden (Beaumont Press 1924).

John Clare: poems chiefly from manuscript edited by Edmund Blunden and Alan Porter, with an introduction by Edmund Blunden (Cobden-Sanderson 1920).

The Poems of John Clare edited by J. W. Tibble, 2 vols (Dent 1935).

Poems of John Clare's Madness edited by Geoffrey Grigson (Routledge & Kegan Paul 1950).

Selected Poems of John Clare edited, with an introduction, by Geoffrey Grigson (Routledge & Kegan Paul 1950).

The Prose of John Clare edited by J. W. and Anne Tibble (Routledge & Kegan Paul 1951).

Selected Poems of John Clare edited, with an introduction, by James Reeves (Heinemann 1954).

The Later Poems of John Clare edited by Eric Robinson and Geoffrey Summerfield (Manchester University Press 1964).

The Shepherd's Calendar edited by Eric Robinson and Geoffrey Summerfield (Oxford University Press 1964).

Selected Poems of John Clare, 1793–1864 chosen by Leonard Clark (E. J. Arnold, Leeds, 1964).

Selected Poems edited by J. W. and Anne Tibble (Dent, Everyman edition 1965).

Selected Poems and Prose edited by Eric Robinson and Geoffrey Summerfield (Oxford University Press 1966); with illustrations by David Gentleman (1967).

The Wood is Sweet; poems for young readers edited by David Powell (Bodley Head 1966).

Selected Poems edited by Elaine Feinstein (University Tutorial Press 1968).

John Clare, Northamptonshire Poet, 1793–1864, selected by J. L. Carr (Kettering 1968–80).

The Penguin Book of English Romantic Verse edited by David Wright (Penguin 1968).

VARIOUS

'John Clare' by G. Claridge Druce in *Northamptonshire Botanologia*, 16, 130, 1912; reprinted in *Flora of Northamptonshire*, Arbroath 1930.

'Reflections on genius' by Thomas Tennant, MD, FRCP, DPM, in *Journal of Mental Science*, xciv, 414, January 1953.

The Birds of John Clare by James Fisher (Kettering and District Naturalists' Society and Field Club 1956).

The John Clare Collection in Northampton Public Library edited by David Powell (County Borough of Northampton 1964).

A Descriptive Catalogue of the John Clare Collection in Peterborough Museum and Art Gallery by Margaret Grainger (Peterborough Museum and Art Gallery 1973).

'Poésie et Folie chez John Clare' by Jean Paira Pemberton, Ph.D thesis, University of Strasbourg 1979.

Poémes et proses de la folie de John Clare présentés et traduit par Pierre Leyris, Suivis de la psychose de John Clare par Jean Fauchette, Mercure de France, Paris, 1969.